AUTHOR'S PREI

This book contains devotional pieces written as a pastoral response to many of the questions, hurts and hopes I encountered in serving five congregations over a period of forty years. As you read and reflect upon them, it is my hope they will bring to you in a living way something of the incomparable blessing that is the life in Christ.

Pastor Mark Anderson
The Season of Advent
2017

DEDICATION

To pastoral mentors upon whose broad shoulders
I have stood through forty years of ministry

and

to the crucible of ministry,
the congregations I have been blessed to serve.

ACKNOWLEDGEMENTS

The origins of this book lie in the first year of my ministry. Several parishioners encouraged me to compile the devotional pieces I was writing for our church newsletter. That encouragement continued from one ministry to another until five congregations later, the project finally took flight. I am deeply grateful to the members of those congregations whose encouragements over the years kept the idea for this book alive.

The precise occasion which provided the context for many of these devotions is no longer known to me. As I have worked with them, however, their ongoing relevance has been sharpened and clarified. I want to thank to Dr. Mark Mattes of Grandview University for his comments on the book and his kind foreward.

Finally, I must offer special thanks to my family. My mother and father, my wife Linda and the 'kids', Kristin (who edited the manuscript), Erik and Geoff. Each in their own way has been an inspiration as I have worked to edit these devotional pieces in the light of our ongoing struggles with faith and life.

FOREWORD

An oasis is a green space in a desert where water can be found to sustain and refresh travelers. Apart from such a place of sustenance it would not be possible for caravan routes to cross the deserts. But with them traders and tourists can be satiated and continue their journeys. Pastor Mark Anderson's daily reflections offer such oases, giving God's grace to sustain us on our earthly journeys. Growing out of decades of pastoral ministry, in the thick and thin of life's ups and downs, Pastor Anderson, like another preacher in the wilderness, John the Baptist, points us to Jesus Christ who is himself life abundant.

Pastor Anderson is a shepherd faithful to the gospel not only in preaching but also in these daily meditations. For those hesitant to trust God because they are afraid God may disappoint, he directs us to Jesus Christ as the unconditional promise of God's faithfulness. For those who feel that they don't need God, that they are sufficient unto themselves, he shows us that only Jesus, as our advocate, can defend us from the accusing law which hounds sinners daily. To those religious people who like the Pharisees of old use their faith as a weapon to attack the broken and weary, he preaches the law, which permits no self-righteousness to define life, and the gospel in which God embraces each sinner. He acknowledges our deep need for rescue because we are all broken and condemned, alienated from God and from one another. But he proclaims an even deeper mercy given to us in Jesus Christ who is God the Father's heart. In Christ, God bears our rejection of his mercy, confronts us with our rejection, and buries our sin in a tomb never to be found again, all so that we might live renewed, in a resurrection life.

Against the stream Pastor Anderson notes that "free will" is but an illusion. We are sinners bound to reject Jesus Christ because we would rather operate by merit and not mercy. Thereby life becomes both a trail of one-up-man-ships and put downs. To such a heartless world, God gives his heart, validates his creation, embraces his prodigals, and sets straight the elder brothers. These devotions, growing out of real life experience interpreted through the lens of scripture, offer no program to help the Christian wayfarer grow in perfection but instead a Person, Jesus Christ, who walks each pilgrim through life, steadying, supporting, and providing fellowship for him or her in the life of the Church.

That God cares for you needs to be heard daily. We need the voice of a preacher for that. In these Christian reflections you receive that voice. You will be blessed and empowered as you read them.

Mark Mattes
Grand View University

"Then Jacob awoke from his sleep and said, "Surely the LORD is in this place, ..." Genesis 28:16

Once there was a farm outside a Minnesota town. The majestic oak tree that stood in the yard, throwing lace-like patterns across the log house, had started life long ago near a path where the Chippewa traveled, their soft moccasins making no sound as they moved through the forested landscape, wildflowers and the seasons. The farmer stumbled behind a team of horses. The morning air was heavy with the smell of earth and animals, sweat and leather as their muscles strained against the plow and the dark earth rolled over. The farmer was close, very close to the land, close to his Bible. He remembered the words of Jacob, "Surely the Lord is in this place...".

Now, in the planting and growing days of spring and summer, the farmland lies buried beneath white-hot asphalt. The oak tree is gone. Airplanes, thunderous with power, have replaced the sounds of cattle lowing and babies waking. The rhythm of the seasons has been replaced, day and night, by restless motion and tight schedules. Does the God of Jacob descend and ascend over neon and suburban sprawl, over cabs and hotels, airports and cities teeming with the trapped, lonely and indifferent masses?

The furious pace of change and its seemingly random, chaotic character is matched by our anxiety and unease. Where do we look for some assurance that the utter despoiling of the world is not our future? The Cross and Resurrection of Christ is where we look. There is no greater desolation than death. Yet God raised Jesus from the dead, thereby planting His promise in the midst of our despoiling and dying. When the Gospel opens our eyes to the amazing grace of Christ, we may awaken from our sleep upon pillows of concrete and steel and exclaim with praise and wonder, "Surely the Lord is in this place...!"

"We were buried therefore with him by baptism into death, so that as Christ was raised from the dead by the glory of the Father, we too might walk in newness of life." Romans 6

It was my first spring in the congregation. David and Debbie shook my hand on Sunday morning after the service and said, "We'll be planting soon. Would you come by and say a prayer?"

A few days later I went to the sanctuary and took the beautiful oak and walnut processional cross out of its stand. After loading it in the back of my pickup, I headed out of town. The streets of Fergus Falls, Minnesota blended away into a landscape of farms, stands of budding trees, and broad fields that stretched to the horizon.

Before long, I rolled to a stop next to a row of huge silver silos. David and Debbie were waiting to greet me. I asked David to take the cross out of the bed of the truck. "Doesn't this belong in church?" he asked. "Yes," I replied, "that's why It's here." We walked, stumbling over clods along the deep furrows, then paused. I planted the cross firmly in the black earth, and we prayed. We gave thanks for life and health, for the good earth, for those who work the soil and their families. We prayed for the safety of David and his workmen, for a productive season and a bountiful harvest. We prayed for those who would be fed by what was grown here. We remembered the words of Jesus that unless a grain of wheat falls into the earth and dies, it cannot live.

When you were baptized you received the sign of the cross so that you might know that wherever you are, there Jesus is. That's His promise to you. And where Jesus is looks like dying and rising, planting and growing, good soil, abundance, "newness of life". He came on a cross so that all avenues would be opened, all impossibilities resurrected. Forgiveness is like that. God comes to us. Jesus plants His Cross, His baptism, willy-nilly, in the thick of living-your living; in fields, offices, schoolrooms, board-rooms and bedrooms, laying claim to sinners where they are, where they live, bringing new life.

"From this time many of his disciples turned back and no longer followed him. 'You do not want to leave too, do you?' Jesus asked the Twelve. Simon Peter answered him, 'Lord, to whom shall we go? You have the words of eternal life." John 6:68

After many years in the pastoral ministry I have reason enough to walk away from the Church. I have seen dishonesty, meanness and duplicity. People have feigned support while privately working to undermine the work of others, including my own. I have seen people driven by the storms of life into the church only to be driven out by the pettiness and indifference of others. At times the Church can seem to be nothing more than a random gathering of touchy, self-interests. So, when I hear from time to time that someone has no time for the Church, I can understand. Believe me.

At the same time I have seen selflessness, sacrifice and compassion. I have witnessed the greatest generosity expressed by those who, at least materially, could least afford it. There are those who have wholeheartedly and without expectations, committed their talents and abilities toward the management of the Church's resources and the good of others. This list could go on.

But as good as people can be, they are not why I believe in the Church or remain in the Church. Neither do I walk out because of all the nonsense. For the picture above is an inconsistent one. The characteristics I have described point to a pattern of unreliability, a picture of instability that encompasses both pastors and people.

When the people's expectations were no longer in line with Jesus and His mission, they began to leave Him. He asked those few around Him if they were also set to bail out. Peter's reply? "Lord, to whom shall we go? You have the words of eternal life."

That is why I stay in the church.

"Do not judge, or you too will be judged...first take the plank out of your own eye, and then you will see clearly to remove the speck from your brother's eye." Matthew 7:1

I have entered a time in life when reminiscing becomes more poignant. I can see far more clearly the days of youth, when I threw myself into the maze of experience, confident that the future was now and that all that mattered was the present. Decades of living and aging have tempered this rashness, until now there is a sobriety and humility about life.

The assertions that drove me to self-hood and independence also turned out to be a willfulness that took me beyond the restrictions and standards meant to keep me safe. They took me into places I should have avoided, and steered my life in ways both great and small into the darkness of grief and heartache. When I began to come to my senses, seeking a solid road of abiding values or an unbroken ascent to a promising future, I discovered that in a thousand ways the downward pull of the world was more than a match. It was then that life became a juggling act of living with the realities of compromise and the tempering of disappointment.

A lot can be said about this, but I want to make a singular point. Far too many people in the Church seem to have little capacity to recognize this struggle in the lives of others, nor do they honestly confront it in themselves. The Church seems often to be a place where it is permissible to come down on the defections of others, thanking God we are not like them, as if we are not bound sinners, locked in our own willfulness and pretensions.

Christian people are to take their cues from the one who went to the Cross, the one who said, "Do not judge, or you too will be judged...first take the plank out of your own eye, and then you will see clearly to remove the speck from your brother's eye."

"God is our refuge and strength, an ever-present help in trouble."
Psalm 46

Martin Luther found a lot to like in the 46th Psalm. As a result he paraphrased its promises and set them to music in the great hymn we know as 'A Mighty Fortress is our God.'

It is not hard to see why Luther held this Psalm in such high regard. The focus is clearly on the mighty, saving acts of God. And this focus became central in that renewal of the Church we call the Reformation. It is still the focus of all who treasure the Gospel above all things.

The great insight of the Lutheran Reformation was nothing novel. Martin simply brought the Gospel message to the forefront, and it did the rest. And as the freedom of the Gospel went to work, it created what it continues to create wherever it is heard: alarm, anger, shock, challenge, joy, freedom, assurance and, in Luther's famous words, "forgiveness of sins, life and salvation. "

The precise occasion of the writing of 'A Mighty Fortress' is not known. What is known is that it came out of Martin's long struggle to know God's peace, a struggle that was brought to rest when the Gospel directed him away from reliance on himself and instead to trust in the mercy of God in Jesus Christ. The confidence and freedom that resulted from this encounter was the singular note that rang throughout the rest of his life. It continues to ring, and joyfully so, in all who find their assurance and hope in the promises of the Gospel.

**"Bear one another's burdens, and so fulfill the law of Christ."
Galatians 6:2**

An elderly visitation pastor returned to the church late one afternoon after a particularly difficult round of visits. In the space of a few hours he had been confronted with sickness, death, marital difficulties, and other serious problems. As he entered the building, slowly making his way toward his study, the young office manger came down the hallway on her way home. She stopped to greet him and as she did so he placed his hand on her shoulder, looked her in the eyes and said,

"Would you do something for me?"
"Of course," she replied.
"Today, the burdens are too great for me", he confessed, "and I fear for my faith. Please tell me Jesus loves me and that my sins are forgiven."

You and I are troubled by many things and at times, we too may fear for our faith. In our sorrows we may forget our Lord Jesus, the "man of sorrows" who is familiar with grief. In our bodily weakness we may forget God's ability to help. We may be inclined to credit our own intelligence and hard work for times of health and prosperity. In these and a host of other ways our weakness of faith, pride, doubt and forgetfulness of God is revealed.

This is why, in our doubts and faithlessness, the Christian is invited again and again to return to God's promises given in Baptism. All of us as God's people may be the bearers of those promises, of the Good News of what God has done for us in Jesus. Even this day you may speak the words that help another Christian to remember what God has graciously done for her, and in the telling help her trust in Him for all her needs, giving renewed strength, joy and confidence to faltering faith.

11

"He does according to His will in the army of heaven, and among the inhabitants of the earth; and no one can stay His hand, or say to Him, 'What are you doing?'..." Daniel 4:35

"Thy will be done," we pray in the Lord's prayer. And it is. In truth, it is God's will that finally matters, for only God's will is truly free. This means that only God's will is pure enough, perfect enough and enduring enough to bring a holy, righteous, unalterable and gracious purpose to all things. To claim such a free will for ourselves, therefore, is nothing short of blasphemy, for it is to claim something that belongs to God alone.

The undiluted witness of the Bible is to the sovereignty of God's Holy will over what we call history. He rules the world with relentless, gracious and almighty power.

Providentially, the Bible tells us that God wills to send the rain upon the just and the unjust, freely extending the blessings of creation to all.

Through the course of time God's will sets up and overthrows all rulers and earthly authorities. Good and evil alike are summoned into the task of governance, for judgment and mercy, where the wicked may be restrained and the benefits of life may be protected and extended.

Within the Church, God's will governs through His Word of law and gospel and the sacraments. Through these He exposes our sin and brings us to know and trust Him in Jesus Christ through the forgiveness of sins, restoring us to Himself and preparing us for an eternal inheritance.

Therefore, I may enter this day with the confidence that God will rule my trembling heart and tentative steps, helping me to grow in the knowledge of faith and freeing me for the capacity to love. I may trust that in all the circumstances of my life, even when I am tested to the extremity of my limits, I am not beyond the working of God's good, holy and gracious will.

"From this time many of his disciples turned back and no longer followed him." John 6:66

We live in an age which demands the popularization of practically everything. This can also extend into the Church and its expressions. Dwindling congregations and shrinking budgets can lead church leaders to sell the birthright of faithfulness for those things that are popular, that simply make us feel good.

Popularized, prosperity religion, however, is inadequate in dealing with the struggles, crosses and losses of our lives. At the same time to proclaim the Cross is not to advocate a religion that simply makes us feel bad. That is no better than its opposite. Rather, we root our proclamation and life in the realism of the Cross because there we are brought up against our actual limits and the goal of our lives in this world.

Therefore, I do not want a church or a preacher who panders to the popular, who simply gives me back to myself in an emotionally comfortable package. I want a church and a preacher who tells me the truth. I want a church and a preacher that tells me Jesus went to the Cross because of me and was raised for me, and because He did I am free to think and pray and feel and hope and struggle my way through the dark, hard and cold places in life. I want a church and a preacher who will tell me that the Christian life is as easy as breathing -and dying.

"I believe that I cannot by my own reason or strength believe in Jesus Christ my Lord, or come to Him; but the Holy Ghost has called me through the Gospel, enlightened me by his gifts, and sanctified and preserved me in the true faith; in like manner as He calls, gathers, enlightens, and sanctifies the whole Christian Church on earth, and preserves it in union with Jesus Christ in the true faith; in which Christian Church He daily forgives abundantly all my sins, and the sins of all believers, and will raise up me and all the dead at the last day, and will grant everlasting life to me and to all who believe in Christ. This is most certainly true."

These words from Martin Luther's Small Catechism, which emphasize our inability to contribute anything of our own – free will, good works, etc. - toward our salvation, shook the Church to its foundations. Luther's words still tend to rile things up. Instead of a religion which emphasizes subjective human cooperation with God in the matter of salvation, the Lutheran Reformation points to the objective work of God in His Word. The content of that Word, written, preached and given in the sacraments is the Gospel of promise and the forgiveness of sins.

The Church in every generation is faced with the task of appropriating the great message of salvation by grace apart from human effort. For every age confronts the Church with the temptation to conform the Gospel to current demands which, in principle, eliminate the Gospel of Grace in favor of some form of self-redemption.

Lutheran Christians, and all who stand with us in this confession, must stand up, even against ourselves, in proclaiming the free gift of salvation; to the benefit of sinners and the Glory of God.

"Remember the Sabbath, and keep it holy." Exodus 20:8

As a youth pastor I spent a lot of time with teenagers. One Sunday evening, following a weekly youth meeting, one of the boys approached me and said he wanted to talk. He was upset with his parents because they would not let him practice sports on Sunday mornings. Instead, they insisted that he worship with them. He asked me to speak with them. I said I would, but that I would tell them to stick to their guns and not let the culture set the agenda.

Some years later, I ran into the young man and his parents at a local restaurant. He had just graduated from college and was starting a new job. He remembered our conversation from years before. At first he was angry, he told me, that I had taken the side of his folks. Now, with college behind him, and sports a thing of the past and playing no role in his life, he was thankful that the witness and influence of his parents gave him what he called the "holy habit" of regular worship.

Some things do not need to be defended. They just need to be said -and done.

"For now we see in a mirror dimly, but then face to face; now I know in part, but then I will know fully just as I also have been fully known. But now faith, hope, love, abide these three; but the greatest of these is love." 1 Corinthians 13:12

On visits as a young boy to Southwestern Minnesota, I recall seeing my great-aunt speaking on an old crank handle wooden telephone. Today, I carry a cell phone. I completed four years of college and four more at the seminary. All my work was hammered out on a typewriter. Today, I work on a computer and do some reading on a tablet. You get the picture. We have become rich in gadgets, in things.

The promise in all of this 'gadgeteering' is that life is supposed to be better. I am not convinced. Just thinking about all the hours I have spent dealing with computer problems is enough to make me long for the simplicity of a typewriter and the reliability of holding a book in my hand. There is that. But I also think the proliferation of things has driven us farther away from one another and from ourselves, in spite of all the fawning over the latest gadget and social media. Many people I talk to, young and old, seem to feel the same way.

When Jesus was asked about the essential business of the human being, His answer was unequivocal: "Love God and your neighbor as yourself." There is nothing here about things. Apart from love, all our scrambling after knowledge and things does make us look rather foolish. An integrated, authentic human life is only possible when love is the center. And that is our dilemma.

In Christ Jesus, God has closed the distance between my lovelessness and His mercy. For the Christian, to be in Christ is to be brought to rest in the knowledge that I am known by God, knowledge that is given as faith, rooted in love. For it is God's inestimable love that integrates my mind and powers, if only dimly for now, that I may know and be known authentically in faith and restored to an authentic humanity.

In the famous Heidelberg Disputation of 1518, Martin Luther set forward the following proposition: "A theologian of glory calls evil good and good evil. A theologian of the Cross calls a thing what it actually is."

What Luther knew is that an inadequate proclamation of the truth results in a theology of self-deception, also known as a theology of glory. The theology of glory fails to acknowledge the profound gravity of sin, and the resulting bondage that determines each generation. And this bondage is principally revealed, as Luther discovered, in the fact that we live under God upon whom we are utterly dependent, and yet against whom we struggle. This is our bondage. When the seriousness of our situation is side-stepped, therefore, there can be no real comfort. Even our religion becomes an enterprise in which we are actually trying to be free of God. For what we are attempting to free ourselves from is God's absolute claim in judgment and mercy upon our lives.

The realization that we do not want God, that we construct numerous defenses against God, including religion, is what the theology of the Cross exposes. In this respect it must do so violently because it moves in on territory that is already occupied by the sinner. This is why we see Baptism not as a symbol of free choice but as the work of the Holy Spirit bringing the death to sin that only God can bring. In order for there to be new life there must be death to the old and that is the last thing we want. That is why Baptism must never be seen as some cute expression of religious culture or a sign of our decision. An actual death occurs and must occur so that the Christ may bring the new person forth on the other side.

The theology of the Cross bears witness to the Gospel not through slick marketing programs, side-show mega-churches or gun-point evangelicalism. The witness to the crucified and risen Lord emerges from within the truthfulness of a Christian community that is honest about its helplessness and bondage, relinquishes all claims, and confesses its' utter dependency upon the grace and mercy of God.

The Greatest Mystery

When I was a young man in the 1960's the "good news of great joy" of which we sang was about the new institutions and movements that seemed bright and promising. We relished throwing out the old and, rather uncritically, embracing the novel.

Now, many years later, all of these institutions have proven themselves to be flawed, delivering as much down side as up side. The hard and gritty realities of life in this world have emerged as the formidable obstacles they truly are; technology has proven to be a poor, soulless substitute for the development of real, human capability and interaction; creeping ignorance continues its march in the face of educational opportunity.

It is easy to be disappointed in such a world, to question God. But do we have that right? After all, who is responsible? All our blaming and finger-pointing just adds to the dysfunction and chaos we have set loose in this place. The One who should really be disappointed is God. What kind of a world does He have to look at?

It would have been easy for Jesus to have finished His prayers in Gethsemane, gotten up, washed His hands of us, and walked out of the garden, out of the city. His thirty or so years in this place were more than enough time to draw the conclusion that there is no deserving here. So why did He do it? Why did He let us kill Him?

The only answer is the greatest mystery of all: God's mercy. Martin Luther observed that in Jesus, God has refused to pull rank on us. That is the mystery. There is nothing more unfathomable in all the Christian faith than this one, simple fact: faced with the enormity of His disappointment, His grief over the mess we have made of this good earth and our lives, God has chosen to have mercy on us. Paul called this salvation by grace, apart from anything we can think, say or do.

In our broken lives and world we receive what we have coming, for this is the harvest of weeds we have sown in the landlord's vineyard. But in Jesus we receive what we do not have coming, what God would give us: pure, unmerited, undeserved grace and mercy. This is the "good news of great joy" of which the angels sang - and so may we.

Watch Out!

The Christmas Festival presents us with familiar characters. Among the supporting cast were the three kings, the wise men. As I reflect on them what strikes me is how their sumptuous gifts and silken robes seemed oddly out of place among the general rudeness of the manger scene. What are these royal intellectuals doing kneeling before a tiny child among animals and crusty shepherds out in the middle of nowhere?

With their gifts and obeisance, the wise men were acknowledging the One to whom their life's obligations, energies and resources now belonged. The picture of kings kneeling is a picture of the transfer of allegiance, loyalty, duty, power. It was to Whom they knelt that matters. Trust, faith, is always defined by its object.

When you and I were baptized, we were given a name: God's name. Our Baptism, among other things, testified to the fact that we now belong to the God who we know as the Father, the Son and the Holy Spirit. Our Baptism was a statement about who we belong to, who has the last word in our lives. For whoever has the last word is our God.

Baptism rearranges our loyalties, transfers our citizenship in such a way that we become the protagonists, representatives, advocates of the kingdom of God. We proclaim "good news of great joy", the reign of life in the midst of the reign of death. This means the shadow of Good Friday always falls over the Christmas manger. For we are not only the beneficiaries of God's reign, we participate in God's reign, which means we are proclaimers of the Cross.

You are not your own. In Baptism God the Father claimed you and gave you the Holy Spirit. The last Word belongs to God. At Christmas, the Christ mass, the Christ worship, you knelt before this God, this same God that was born to an unwed mother, surrounded by animal dung, smelly shepherds and kings who radically altered their allegiance. Watch out! If this is the God who has taken hold of you in Baptism, who has the last word in your life, you just know that whatever life He has in store for you is not going to be business as usual!

Unloving Critics, Uncritical Lovers

The expression 'radical inclusion' is used in some Christian circles to describe the character of God's grace. If radical inclusion describes grace, perhaps it would be useful to clarify just what grace actually is.

We may also ask, what kind of life does this radical grace make possible? To put a fine point on it, grace makes it possible for us to take responsibility for our past, without condemnation, even as we assume new responsibilities as servants of God in the love and freedom grace makes possible. We are able to confess our sins and walk in a new life because of grace.

This means that the Church, the community of grace, is not a judgmental community. But we are an admonishing community.

The problem with some uses of radical inclusion to describe grace is that grace is actually being defined as 'indulgence,' anything goes. Grace becomes an excuse for expanding the God-imposed limits on our humanity into areas where there is no freedom. If I indulge you, whether I really care about you is questionable. Good parents don't indulge their children's every whim unless they want to produce selfish, willful brats. Indulgence is not saying 'I love you.' It is saying, "Go ahead, do what you want. I don't care."

The Church is a community of grace, a community of forgiveness and love. And because love is our aim, our way with one another is to care. And when you care, you admonish. And to admonish is to express warning or disapproval in a gentle, friendly and concerned manner. Admonition is not unloving criticism. Without admonition a very important aspect of love within the Christian community is not expressed, and at great cost. Love is not lazy, nor does it overlook the harm we may cause one another. Christians are neither unloving critics nor uncritical lovers.

There are any number of issues in church life that are defended in the name of radical inclusion. But it is fair to ask, in fact in the name of Christian love it must be asked, if radical inclusion really means nothing more than indulgent acquiescence to willfulness insisting on its own way. If this is what is actually meant, it surely cannot be grace. Nor can it rightly be called love. In fact, it can hardly be called Christian.

Culture Myths

Our faith is a salvation story. The culture has salvation stories also. Turn on your television or go to the movies and you will find all kinds of salvation stories. Law and order stories are very popular in this respect. Detectives, CSI operatives and James Bond take on the evil threats within society and, in the end, our confidence and optimism are more or less restored. Sci-fi travelers encounter monsters from an alien darkness but manage to push back the darkness, and our optimism is again restored. Even if there is no God in the mix, these myths tells us that we can roll up our own sleeves and bring about something resembling salvation.

Cultural salvation myths create two kinds of people: you are part of the solution or part of the problem. This is very much how the Jewish Pharisees of Jesus time saw their fellow Jews with respect to the Roman occupiers. God would deliver Israel, provided everyone obeyed God's commandments and lived righteously.

Now you can get some idea as to what the Pharisees were saying when they accused Jesus of being a friend of sinners. He was giving encouragement to the people who were part of the problem, not the solution. But what was actually going on in Jesus? The "sinners" who encountered Jesus encountered grace, a new and different way of being in the world. Perhaps they were part of the problem according to pious Judaism, obstacles to the survival of Israel. But in these dramatic actions of actually befriending people who were part of the problem, Jesus was staking out a different vision of salvation. His parables and teachings were insights that point to a new vision: the vision of grace. Grace was the radical vision that was now at work in Him. The life, death and resurrection of Jesus are the basis in history upon which Christians speak of the reality of grace. In Jesus grace has actually happened.

For those who place their trust, their faith in the culture myths of law and order, grace is an idle vision, a luxury that can have no place in the "real world." But to place trust, faith, in the event of Jesus, to entrust yourself to this Lord, is to proclaim that nothing is more real, more trustworthy in the real world than the grace of God.

Why?

The Book of Genesis tells of the flood which destroyed a sinful humanity. When it was over, God made a promise that He would never take such action again. In other words, God imposed upon Himself a restraint, a limit. No matter how evil humanity was, God's way with the world would not be to overpower it with force. The innocent suffering and death of Jesus are the clearest expression of God's intent to enter into and participate in the suffering of the world. This way of facing suffering and evil, the Bible tells us, has broken the power of evil, anticipating the end of suffering. Still, human freedom will be misused and abused and certain kinds of suffering will be the result.

The 'why' questions that come out of such suffering do not all run in the direction of God. Asking 'why' can also serve to mobilize human efforts to address the conditions and circumstances that resulted in such terrible suffering and death. For there are many instances of suffering that have little mystery attached to them. The causes may be discerned and solutions reached.

There is also the question of what we do with suffering. How do we handle it? Do we simply shake our fists at the heavens, lamenting in grief and bitterness? There is a place for that, no doubt. At the same time, suffering can take us outside of ourselves and into the suffering of others. Suffering can make us more aware of the fragile, vulnerable character of life and motivate us to stand with others in their suffering, while seeking ways to alleviate it.

There are no risk-free zones in this life. Suffering can and will be a companion. As we ask the tough questions of God and of ourselves it may be helpful to look again at the Cross and the man there who also cried out, "Why?" For there we see not only a fragile man who walked in faith with God, we also see a tender God, who walks in faith with men and women.

This insight does not exhaust the meaning of the Cross, to be sure. Jesus death, after all, was a sacrifice for sin, the end of the law, and no mere example of love. At the same time, the Cross reveals, in the deepest sense, the God who knows and participates in our suffering.

NIKE

The Christian faith does not have a calendar which uniquely plots historical progress. What we do have is the New Testament Book of Revelation, which some have used as a lens through which events and time are viewed, usually with embarrassing, even tragic consequences for those who have tried to pin down dates, events and times. Those who have taken it upon themselves to predict the future have largely misread the book and its' meaning.

For example, when we put the question, "What does it reveal?" to the Book of Revelation, what kind of answer should we expect? Is it a collection of hidden clues, like some ancient 'Da Vinci Code,' just waiting for the right sleuth to unlock its mysteries? If so, then the countless number of misreadings that have resulted would seem to indicate that we have yet to find just the right key.

I want to suggest that the reading of history we receive in this book is clear, straightforward and promising. The very first words in the book tell us what to expect: the book is a revelation of Jesus Christ. The book goes on in the first chapter to amplify various ways in which we may know Him, experience Him and trust Him. Events associated with Christ are also mentioned, but they are not the subject. Christ Jesus is the subject. If we may draw a reading of history from this book it would be this; history is Christ-centered.

The Book of Revelation is frank and realistic about the suffering faith encounters in this life. It tells us that as history moves toward its climax we may expect to see a hardening of the lines of battle, where the godless will say no with firmness, bitterness and ugliness.

We know that it is Christ's suffering, displayed in crucified weakness, that in the end saves us. At the same time the Book of Revelation assures the Church that the power of the resurrected Christ is equal to anything Satan can send against Him. We can see this in the most commonly recurring verb in the entire book, the verb 'nike,' to conquer. This word refers both to the Christian who conquers the world through faith and to Jesus Christ, the Conqueror, the One who will finally deliver His people from the demonic powers of catastrophe and meaninglessness.

The Lens of the Cross

As a Lutheran Christian I read the Bible in the light of my Baptism, in the light of the Cross. For in baptism my old self is put to death with Christ and raised to new life with Him. This means that to encounter God's Word, whether in judgment or mercy, will always be to encounter the *living* God. To have God's grace in Christ means that the Word of Scripture will only be a threat to my old self-justifying self, not to the new person who is being brought along in Christ Jesus, who is justified by grace alone. When I read the Bible in the light of this unconditional grace, I may begin with the assumption that this Word of God is both for me and against me.

To be let in on God's grace means that I am free to join Him in His judgments on the old person within me. For the new person in Christ in me, who trusts in God's grace alone, does not want the old self to be let off the hook. I am actually anxious to see the old boy put in his place! Since there is no condemnation in Christ, I can face all accusers: "You cannot say anything about me that I have not already said about myself." The Word of God is only the adversary of the old, sinful person in me.

But more than adversary of sin, the Word of God is advocate for sinners. This means that when I read and study the Bible I am encountering the one who is for me. If you want to know what God thinks about you, do not look at your bank account, health, history or nature. And do not look at your sins. Look at Jesus Christ on the Cross. There, you see God condemning the sin in you and taking you up in His grace and forgiveness. The entire Bible is the story of this God who confronts sin for us that He may be grace for us. When we read the Bible through the lens of the Cross, we encounter God not as threat but as grace, and our lives are set free to trust.

If you have been reluctant, even averse, to picking up your Bible, I encourage you to reconsider. Make the Cross alone your lens of interpretation. And as you read, you may be confident that your merciful God will be keeping the promise of your baptism, putting the old self-justifying you away with the crucified Jesus, even as He works to bring the new justified you to life, in the freedom of faith, with your resurrected Lord.

Free and Obedient

Our American way of life may reinforce the dreams of the rugged individual but self-governance is a fiction where the Christian life is concerned. Christ has made of us a people created for the obedience of faith, not a loose gathering of little kings and queens, intent on ruling the petty kingdoms of the self. The pressures we feel upon us in daily life to be good for something, to contribute, to care for our neighbor and the world are not the soulless powers of an indifferent universe. Those pressures are the living, active power and will of God at work through His law acting on us and all people. The Holy Spirit and the Word are not casual bystanders.

It may sound surprising, but the main characteristic of the life of our Savior was not love or compassion or caring. Those things were there in abundance, to be sure. What the New Testament witness is anxious to report as of prime significance is that Jesus was obedient to the will of His Father. He lived under the pressures and obligations of God's Law, just as we must. But unlike us, His obedience to God's good and gracious intention for Him never wavered.

The paradox of the Christian life is that you and I have been set free for obedience. We have been cut loose in order to be bound up again, lifted to our feet only to kneel once more. Martin Luther described it this way: "The Christian is a free lord, subject to none. The Christian is a dutiful servant, subject to all." Christ's singular obedience to the Father, for us, resulted in His death and our freedom from sin. At the same time, that "obedience that comes from faith," according to which we now live, is meant to guide us, to send us back into the battle, in a grateful obedience to the Father. As the Christian attends to the Word of God, our allegiance is directed away from sin and self toward reliance on His grace, which is another way of saying God summons us to resume the primary role for which we were created and re-created in Christ-a free and joyful obedience to the Father that is expressed in caring for the neighbor and the creation.

Murphy's Law

We are all familiar with Murphy's Law: "If something can go wrong it will go wrong." Or there are those famous commentaries on Murphy's law: "Murphy was an optimist" and, "If you think things are getting better, look again!" We can chuckle over such unvarnished pessimism but it has a very long history in the Church.

Traditional Lutheran language about sin has emphasized the totality of our sinfulness. The older service of confession and forgiveness spoke of our being "sinful and unclean." Nowadays, some use the language of being in "bondage to sin." In either case, the Lutheran tradition has wanted to take sin seriously. But this emphasis on the sinfulness of humanity also has caused problems. Many of us remember a Lutheran Church that constantly reinforced the sinfulness of people to the extent where there was simply no point in looking for anything good. What was actually a very important biblical and theological emphasis became quite destructive, psychologically, of many peoples' self-understanding.

At the same time, the more liberal side of the Church has also turned the wheel hard over in favor of the generosity of reason, shifting its focus away from the gravity of sin, and our need for a gracious God, to our need to have and to be gracious neighbors. Good will and fairness will create a just and peaceful world because all of us essentially good and well-intentioned people want it to be so. Everything is affirmed, nothing is out of bounds. Unconditional affirmation will bring a glorious new day. This may be psychologically easier to swallow, but under this view the gravity of sin is minimized and may be denied altogether.

Our bottom line is that salvation comes by God's grace in Christ, apart from human goodness or effort. Such trust does not deny human goodness and its role in the immediate future. Rather, such trust affirms that it is God's gracious goodness alone that will bring the ultimate future.

The External Promise

A young man came to see me who had been raised in the Lutheran Church but was now active in a non-denominational community. He had come on a mission to repudiate his baptism as an infant. I expressed my happiness at his new-found enthusiasm for Jesus and suggested that there might be another way to think about this.

I suggested that we were looking at a question that ran in two directions. Does baptism necessarily lead us to think primarily about ourselves or about God? Does Christian religious experience take us outside of ourselves or send us into ourselves?

I suggested that the experience of God leads not into an interior experience of the self but to a comprehension of God who comes to us in the external word of promise. The Lutheran response to the God who comes to us in His grace is not to write an autobiography but to point beyond and outside ourselves to God. It is not my perceived experience of God that is decisive. What is decisive is God's word of promise to me and for me.

Your Baptism as an infant, I said to him, was never meant to underline your experience of God but to point to God being for you. It began a God-initiated life and dialogue. His feeling that something was perhaps lacking in his experience as a Christian was simply an expression of the human side of that dialog with God. For in our experience of living we more often than not keenly feel the depth of our need, perhaps even God's absence. The faithful response at such times, however, is not to look inward but to move away from self-consciousness toward your baptism. For Baptism is a gracious reminder that you are God's adopted child. Baptism is an ongoing promise-event. Baptism declares that your life moves in and with Christ Jesus in a never-ending dialogue where the wavering and wandering words and feelings of your quite unreliable experience are always answered by the utterly reliable Word of God's grace.

"If you are the Son of God, come down from the cross!"
Matthew 27:40

He did not come down, of course, and this was proof enough for them that all God-talk where Jesus was concerned was bunk. It never occurred to them that the deepest, clearest revelation of God for humans was right there in the ripped flesh, blood and death.

Much of the onward and upward religion of today has ruled out this stark definition in favor of what people have always clamored for: an onward and upward, positive, uplifting, fulfilling and glory-filled God. Churches everywhere are throwing ladders against the walls of heaven, scrambling to free themselves from the bondage, suffering and confusion of the world, storm the halls of glory and grab a piece of divinity. But all this does is diminish God's very self-revelation, the place where He wants to be known, and render the Cross of Jesus useless.

The proclamation of the Crucified Jesus for us in Word and sacrament must be the singular point of contact for us. This is because there is no pre-existing point of contact in us, no spark of divinity which God fans like a sad ember into a roaring flame of faith and love. We must be met where we actually are, in the utter deadness of sin with no possibility in ourselves. God must become sin and death for us in order that He may be life for us.

This means that the Christian life may have little to do with the glory and praise religion of God-seeking. In this life there will be no heaven ahead of time. Jesus did not die between two gilded candles on an altar, or in the midst of a hyper-ventilating praise band. He died between two criminals like you and me. That is still where he wants to be found, in the company of real sinners distinguished only by the knowledge of their great need.

The Gospel of the crucified God grounds the Christian in the real world of hurts and hopes and releases us from delusional spiritual pursuits so that we may be what we were intended to be: creatures who are content to be engaged in the practical affairs of daily living in that radical cross-carrying faith that is content to entrust the things of God, to God, expecting nothing, as we await with Advent-longing the future that God has promised.

Church for People Who Don't want Church

I have been in the Church long enough to have survived various expressions of the lust for worship relevancy: the tumultuous sixties when liturgical babies were flying out with the bathwater, the somnambulant seventies when "I'm OK, You're Ok," became a new gospel for the self in search of itself. Recent decades have seen many in the churches embarrassingly succumb to the American penchant for marketing solutions, convincing themselves that the only way to grow the church is to give people a church for people who don't want church.

A well-known mega-church practitioner of this brand of religion started his church by going door to door and asking people what they didn't like about traditional churches. Apparently, he felt that mounting an assault on traditional Christian expressions of worship was a valid component of evangelism. Predictably, he got the usual responses: don't like organs, don't like liturgy, don't like candles, don't like robes, don't like hymnals, don't like stained glass, and on and on the list went. So, he proceeded to offer a church built around all these negative assessments, giving people exactly what they did want, themselves. And that is the problem.

Over long centuries, the traditions of Christian worship developed in part to remove the self from the center of life. I have believed for a long time that this is precisely what many sense is happening to them in the formal structure of traditional worship. They are removed from the center. And they do not like it one bit. Maybe you do not either.

The formal structure of traditional Christian worship places God at the center, not the self. This is what it intends to do and is one of the best things it can do for you. When churches provide church for people that do not want church they do them no favors. Christian worship ought to assist the self in finding a back seat as it identifies with the larger community of saints, gathered in the presence of Word and sacrament. Most importantly, Christian worship is an invitation to enter, in wonder, love, praise, thanksgiving, and humility the ineffable, profound mystery of God's love and forgiveness in Jesus Christ.

"For by one Spirit we were all baptized into one body -- Jews or Greeks, slaves or free -- and all were made to drink of one Spirit." 1Corinthians 12:13

Many people have an aversion to what they call 'organized religion.' It is a bit puzzling, if you think about it. Can you name any regular activity or gathering of human beings that is not organized in some way? The objection to the organized character of religion cannot be aimed at being organized.

The objection to organized religion, it seems to me, prefers to assert the individual over the community. This is really no surprise in a culture where the individual is sovereign. No wonder independent Americans have taken to an internalized, experiential form of religion which seeks God within the self. I have heard people say that all they need is a personal relationship with Jesus and that being part of a church community does not matter.

To claim that all that matters is a personal relationship with God is to deny how God Himself has defined the character of the Christian life. "We were all baptized into one body," the Bible says. Oops! There is that nasty word "we". Like it or not, if you have been given the Holy Spirit, you belong with all those who share that Spirit. To be Christian is to be baptized into a community of faith.

So, here is some advice. Forget spiritual naval-gazing or traveling down that dead end road called personal experience. The only god you will find there is one of your own making. If you want to know what being in the Spirit is all about, look around you at the folks in church on Sunday morning who have gathered around Word and sacrament. This messy, inconvenient bunch of baptized sinners may not fit with your personalized view of religion, but it is definitely God's idea of what it means to be Church. He has organized it that way.

Repetition and Meaning

We resist repetition. Those in the marketing business figured this out long ago. So, they continually assist us in fleeing repetition by offering us the next big thing, variety, change.

This formula keeps working, because most of what we consume in this constant diet of change does not satisfy. In fact, it leads to increased restlessness and boredom. What this ought to reveal to us is that we do not fight boredom with constant change.

This insatiable desire to flee boredom has infected the worship of many churches. The objection "It's boring," is a common complaint. Actually, the issue is not that worship is boring. The issue which ought to be confronted in those who voice this complaint is why should the church become an accomplice in your restless efforts to relieve yourself of boredom?

All life is repetition. Daily life is made up of all kinds of repetitive patterns, habits, and rituals. We address boredom not by mindlessly chasing the new, but by investing meaning into repetition. If you cannot see the depth of meaning and value in the little repetitions, the little liturgies of daily life, do not expect meaning to result from your efforts to run from them.

My grandmother, Ruth, started each day by spending time with her Bible. This was something she practiced all of her life. After her time with the Scriptures, she went on with her day. The activities she had planned rarely changed: shopping on one day, laundry on another and so forth. I lived with her for a time after my grandfather died. She never struck me as someone who was bored with the ordered life she lived. In the simple, repetitive tasks of daily living, she saw greater meaning. Her life was tuned to the Word of God and she met each day anticipating that Word from Him whose mercy makes all things new.

"See what love the Father has given us, that we should be called children of God; and that is what we are." 1John 3:1

After the prodigal son had returned home, he may have had second thoughts. He may have wished for a forty hour week instead of being restored to the rights of a son. Now that he was home, the full weight and obligation of being a son were upon him. He once again carried the pressures of his freedom and the responsibility of bearing the family name.

For all the moaning and complaining that comes from those who take a paycheck from an employer, the fact remains that most people do not want the responsibilities, burdens, and obligations of ownership. The majority are quite content to punch the clock and then walk away from the job at the end of the week, thanking God it is Friday.

Many also prefer an employee/employer relationship with God. It is easier that way. Provide me with a job description and then give me what I have coming. Those who practice an employer/employee version of the Christian faith are probably more in tune with the prodigal son's elder brother. He stayed at home, complained about his brother's lack of work ethic and his moral laxity, did what he was told, and demanded his rights. But this is not the scenario which describes sons and daughters of God's kingdom.

In Jesus Christ, God has not simply adjusted our job description. God has completely altered our status. This new status is the gift of your Baptism. The New Testament uses the language of royalty to describe what it means to be a child of God. Sons and daughters of royalty do not punch clocks. They freely share the benefits and obligations of their high status.

The Christian has entered a kingdom of grace, not a business relationship. There is nothing to earn, nothing to prove. Christ has done it all. To live within the kingdom is to know the freedom of royal sons and daughters. To rule within the kingdom is to serve in love.

Martin Luther put it this way, "The Christian is a free lord, subject to none. The Christian is a dutiful servant, subject to all."

Psalm Places

Once there was a woman who stood in the doorway of a farmhouse in Iowa. She leaned heavily on the frame, her hand over her mouth, not so much fighting back tears as waiting for them to come. Her son placed his bags in the trunk of the old Chevy and slammed the lid shut. With one last wave and a smile, he got in the car. His father started the engine and drove away from the house down the long the dirt driveway, made a dusty turn and disappeared, swallowed by the tall corn. Her little boy was gone, really gone. He was off to war.

The tears were coming now. She watched for a long time, still feeling his embrace, his kiss on her cheek, his words of reassurance. Finally, she turned on the old oak floor. The screen door clapped quietly behind her as she slowly walked to the kitchen, sat down at the table and opened her Bible. She turned to the Psalms. She searched and found words that came from someone else, long ago, who sought comfort. Now these words sought her: pleading words, words heavy with concern, seeking protection and guidance for one who was loved. As she read, she prayed. The psalmists words and her words became one.

There are stories behind the Psalms. Sometimes this simple insight eludes us. Hurts and hopes, joys and sorrows gave birth to these words. A man struggles with the loss of friendship and betrayal; a warrior gives thanks for victory after the sweat, blood, and terror of battle; a thankful priest, pens words of thanksgiving. And there are laments. Most of the psalms, the majority, in fact, are laments. Sorrows, fears, griefs, anger, and bitterness pour out of them like a flood-the same way they pour out of you and me when we are in those places.

I call these 'Psalm Places,' these times and places when we search for words to express the depth of our faith, or lack of it, the depth of our feeling.

If the Living Word of God would come in the lament of the psalmist, and if that same Word would sit at the kitchen table with a weeping woman on a late summer day, in a small farmhouse in Iowa, then that Word will meet you in your 'Psalm Places,' too.

"Forgetting what lies behind and straining toward what is ahead, I press on toward the goal for the prize for the upward call of God in Christ Jesus." Philippians 3:13

As life moves on we accumulate memories. Some memories remain with us like cherished friends, giving comfort, encouragement, and filling the present with an ongoing sense of fulfillment.

Others may haunt us and tinge our lives with sadness, melancholy and guilt. Of these some are rooted in troublesome or tragic events that were beyond our control. A natural disaster struck. The stock market plunged and assets were wiped out. A medical condition fundamentally altered the course of life. Events like these may leave us reeling in an effort to regain our balance, but we feel no remorse. We did not cause them.

Some memories are of wrongs done to you by others. Someone you once loved rejected you for another. A business associate cheated you. Someone close to you violated a confidence. Rising above the resulting bitterness or anger may be difficult but the fault, in the end, is not yours.

But there are still other memories. These are the memories of the wrongs you have done. They demand you deal with them. They are on your hands.

We have all left a debris field of wrongs in the wake of our lives. And try as we might, we will never clear the wreckage of our past. These deeds follow us and accuse us. What will we do?

Saint Paul urges us to forget it all. But, you may object, surely this is too simplistic. Memories are not that easy to put away. This is true. But Paul dares to invite us to forget, because those haunting memories now belong to Christ Jesus. He paid for them on His Cross.

Giving your sins to Christ Jesus will not remove the scars. But the open wounds of guilt and remorse will be closed and healed. For once Christ Jesus took your sins upon Himself, He stripped them of all the accusation they contained. It is as if those things of which you are ashamed never happened. Now you are free-free to bask in the good memories of your past even as you press on toward the glorious future God has prepared for His people!

"Everyone who drinks of this water will thirst. The one who drinks of the water I shall give will never thirst." John 4:12-14

Once there was a traveler who lost himself in a vast, uncharted wilderness. He survived, just barely, on insects and the drops of dew he could lick off plants in the early mornings. After a long time he settled in to this life. Being parched and always on the edge of hunger became normative for him. Then one day he came upon a pool of water in a dark ravine between towering cliffs. His deep thirst was awakened and drove him into the water where he drank his fill. Only when it was too late, as he lay dying, did he realize that the water was brackish, poisonous. There was no guide, familiar with the wilderness, to warn him away.

The wilderness is the world in which we find ourselves. An arid world that has stolen its existence from God. The traveler is anyone who inhabits this wilderness, believing that any diet that feeds the senses is life-giving. The poisonous waters are those false promises offered up to those who are unable to discern the difference between God's Word of life and words that promise life but deliver death.

Yes, there are powers in the brackish waters. And they mean us no good. If all that the Church can offer up against these powers are the non-redemptive affects of prosperity preaching, consultants on church growth, programs that meet our so-called needs, marketing strategies to increase sales (fill the pews), smug, middle class morality or the call to moral effort, we are done for.

What we need is a Redeemer, a Savior we can trust who discerns our real thirst and can guide us to living water. In Baptism, by the water and the Word, we are brought into just such a redemptive, life-giving relationship with God in Christ.

Drink from any other source and continued thirst will be your fate, even unto death. Drink from Christ Jesus, in Word and sacrament, and He will be for You, according to His promise, "a well of water springing up to eternal life."

"Where can I go from your Spirit? Where can I flee from your presence? If I go up to the heavens, you are there; if I make my bed in the depths, you are there." Psalm 139:7

Positivism, humanism, materialism. These three 'isms' are the defining philosophical systems of our age and probably of your life, whether you know it or not. What they add up to is this: if you cannot taste it, touch it, see it, hear it or do something with it, it isn't real. The orientation of modern life is to what is. Beyond this arid view of reality everything else is nothing but speculation or fantasy. With so many millions actually believing this, it is no wonder that a current popular statement of this faith-or lack of it- is contained in one word: 'whatever.' If the tangible is all there is, then all we are is, well, dirt. Nothing really matters. Whatever.

Yet the entire witness of Holy Scripture is to a creation infused with Spirit. The people of Israel, for example, took spirituality very seriously. It was in the fiber of their being. In waking and sleeping and walking, in conceiving and bearing children, in planting and harvesting, work and rest, in war and peace, in all aspects of life the numinous, the spiritual, was most real.

The Scriptures witness to a God who married dirt with spirit. One or the other will not do. The creation is a coming together of the material and Spirit. There is no more obvious display of this than the Incarnation of God in Jesus the Christ. "The Word became flesh and lived among us...".

The material does not derive meaning from itself. The Spirit gives meaning to the material. There is no 'there' where you are not in the presence of the Spirit. There is no hiding place. This is what the psalmist was observing in the text. This view of reality gives real meaning to the creation, where our lives, and all their works and all their ways, are displayed on the stage of sacred history.

"And the Word became flesh, and dwelt among us, and we saw His glory, glory as of the only begotten from the Father, full of grace and truth." John 1:14

Translations vary but there are roughly 800,000 words in the Bible. How many events do these words represent? I have never seen a statistic for that, but it is more important than the number of words. The event within the words is the thing. How many events are there in the Bible? Are some more important than others? Where did they come from? Where do they go? I knew a man once who closed his eyes and tried to imagine himself through the stories of the Bible. Who is the power within the event, behind the words?

The 800,000 words of the Bible are one event, distilled into many stories. That is how real people live and do theology. We inhabit stories, seamlessly, then we struggle to make the story known. If you were asked to say what you believe, you would not recite disembodied facts. You would tell your story.

Before anything was made the Word was. That is a Bible story. How do you tell your children about the Word within and beyond all words, the Word that was and is and will be? Words always want to go to where they were before the words. All the tenses are senses that precede the words, like someone who pushes a child on a swing, or someone who pushes ink onto paper, or Someone who speaks and something is created out of nothing. What matters is the mind, the power, the reality behind, beneath, in, under and with the words and the event.

Events are words and words are events. That is biblical. The Word in the flesh, the Word in Baptism, the Word in Holy Communion, the Word in Gospel speaking are events of the Word. They are one Word. They are spoken events, spoken against abstraction, God expressing Himself, making the story of your life and the story of Jesus one, interpreted by grace and truth.

Dr. Jekyl and Mr. Hyde

It is time once again for your day in court - and mine. Martin Luther, reflecting on the Biblical picture of man and woman, recognized that we are two selves, a kind of Dr. Jekyl and Mr. Hyde. One self is lawless, motivated by ego and a thousand impulses. The other, the new person in Christ, delights in the law of the Lord, finds its refuge and joy in Him. Luther, like Paul before him, recognized that throughout this life these two selves are at war with one another. You can see it, feel it, in your own life as well.

As a result, Luther characterized the Christian life as a daily return to Baptism, a daily return to repentance, a daily return to the court of God's law where we stand before the bench and are given opportunity to be indicted once again. The old rascal in us must be undone, condemned and led to the place of execution, to the Cross, to Baptism, there to be crucified with Christ.

At the same time, even as the old sinful, self is executed with Christ so is the new person raised with Him in Baptism. We are brought from the Cross to the empty tomb. All things are made new. The past is gone, a new day has come. Just as the old sinner in us delights in lawlessness and the promotion of the self, the new person in Christ finds delight in love and trust. In Christ we become servants and friends of one another. Our joy and delight are in God and His grace.

The old sinner in me trembles at the thought of standing before the bench. The new man in Christ, however, anxious to be free, cannot wait to be dragged into court!

So, as I begin this new and untried day, bring down the gavel, Lord! Send me to the cross that I may die with Christ and be raised with Christ into the freedom and joy of Your kingdom!

"...you, though a wild olive shoot, have been grafted in among the others and now share in the nourishing sap from the olive root..."
Romans 11:17

A plum can grow on a peach tree. It does not happen naturally, of course. Grafting is necessary. A twig from a plum tree is carefully inserted into a branch of a peach tree. The tree remains a peach tree but it bears plums on the grafted twig.

The Bible uses this image as an example of the relationship between Christ and believers. Saint Paul, in his letter to the Romans, says they are grafted into Christ as an olive shoot is grafted into a good root. Saint John describes Christ as the vine giving life to its branches.

When we are grafted into Christ through Baptism we do not become divine, just as the plum twig does not become a peach twig. But the plum twig draws all its' life from the tree.

It is a great miracle of God that we may be be grafted into divinity and partake of the very life of God though Christ.

"No human eye has ever seen God: the only Son, who is in the Father's bosom--He has made Him known." John 1:18

A friend of mine had a word for much of what passes for preaching. He called it 'bird watching.' According to bird watching preachers, God is essentially a conundrum, a mystery to be discussed, a curiosity about whom little can concretely be said. Birdwatcher theology points off into the cosmos and says things like, "My, isn't that interesting. Who knows? God could be this or God could be that. God is in everything. All religions are essentially the same. No religion has a corner on Truth." You get the picture.

The Biblical witness is not so timid-or spineless-where God is concerned. Every page of the Bible concerns itself with revelation, with making God known. In fact, the essential message of the Bible is this: God is speaking.

For those who genuinely seek God this ought to come as good news. Light has entered the darkness. God has expressed Himself in such a way as to be beyond all ambiguity. This revelation culminated in the coming of Jesus, the human face of God. "The Word became flesh and dwelt among us...." But it is precisely the concreteness of the revelation in Jesus that offends the generosity of our reason, which we may use to keep God at arm's length.

My late friend went on to say that we should expect this from the world but when the preachers of the Church demonstrate this same offense it is time for them to seek alternative forms of employment. Finally, he had a suggestion. Every pulpit should have a sign clearly visible to pastor and people which reads,"No Bird watching Allowed".

**"Unless the LORD build the house, they labor in vain that build it."
Psalm 127:1**

My maternal grandfather was a building contractor in Minneapolis. After coming here, from Norway early in the 20th century, he worked building barns in North Dakota. Eventually he moved to the Twin Cities and started his own construction business.

All my grandfather's carpenters were Norwegians and for many years every house was built by hand-no power tools were allowed.

My mother's cousin was one of those carpenters and he told her once why he liked working for my grandfather. "Where other builders use three nails," he said, "your father uses five." All the homes they built are still standing, sturdy as ever.

In a temporal, transitory life, even our finest efforts cannot stand against the ravages of time. After all, my grandfather's houses, as well-built as they are, will one day be torn down.

The Psalmist, reflecting on the work of the Lord, recognized that only those plans laid down by the Living God will endure. And God has made this plan known: through the power of the Gospel the framework of faith, hope and love are built upon Christ, the sure foundation. In Baptism God has established us upon this foundation, and the gates of hell will not prevail against it.

"The true light has come into the world." John 1:9

On a warm summer night in Wisconsin, a lone firefly made its' appearance among the shrubs near my father's house. I watched for a few minutes, but no other fireflies appeared, result of dry spring and summer weather.

That one small light was enough to penetrate the gathering darkness of the evening, but its erratic course, as it flitted here and there, made it difficult to follow. Eventually it faded from view and was gone. All that remained was the darkness.

Many have come promising light; Adolf Hitler spoke of a brilliant future for the German people and proceeded to plunge them and most of the world into darkness. The Marxists promised a bright future to the Russians, Chinese and others, and gave them terror, death, and subjugation on an unprecedented scale.

John writes of the "true light" that has come into the world. That true light is God's Living and abiding Word, Jesus Christ. For now, we follow Him in faith, traveling a course that is unerring, straight and true. No darkness can overcome it. One day we will live fully in His light. No lesser lights will be required. The one, glorious light of Christ will be enough to flood the eternal vistas of heaven.

"I have been crucified with Christ and I no longer live, but Christ lives in me. The life I live in the body, I live by faith in the Son of God, who loved me and gave himself for me." Galatians 2:9

A seasoned parish pastor once reflected on what he thought were the ten most important things to keep in mind regarding parish ministry. The very first and most important point was this: nothing works. As a young pastor, I found this startling and unconvincing. I still thought something was possible.

He went on to say that many people are disillusioned with the Church because they approach it with a faulty expectation. Namely, that religion is supposed to make life work. Faith sees things differently.

The Christian life is defined by Baptism, not our expectations, realism not idealism. Paul tells us in Roman 6 that Baptism is, first and foremost, a participation in the death of Christ. It is an invitation to dying as a way of life. We have been crucified with Christ. Our life and the world are not progressing, they are being brought to end.

At the same time, we have been raised with Christ in Baptism. It is no longer we who live but Christ who lives in us. Our wagons are hitched to Christ Jesus and the future that He alone will bring. This is a great promise of the Gospel.

Our short-sighted expectations, constantly on the hunt for solutions, can only lament that in the midst of life we die. Faith, on the other hand, has no such expectation, but receives the life that is given, rejoicing that in the midst of death we live!

"God was in Christ reconciling the world to Himself." 2 Corinthians 5:19

On the face of it, the crucifixion of Jesus was one more example of an innocent man unjustly condemned. But the symbol of the Cross, and the church buildings over which it has been lifted are not meant to merely signify a noble death. There have been many noble deaths throughout history. What's different about this one?

As the early Christians took up their life in the wake of Jesus life, death, resurrection and ascension, the Holy Spirit gradually revealed to them unfolding dimensions of Christ's death. Paul's summation captured something essential: "God was in Christ reconciling the world to Himself." The Church continues to proclaim the meaning of the Cross, the very fact of it, as central to the faith. The following are three aspects of that proclamation.

The cross is a window into the nature of God, addressing our blindness. The Cross reveals to us that God is more than an all-powerful cosmic engineer designing and creating worlds. Through the Cross, God has revealed both the magnitude of our sin and the depth of His mercy.

The Cross represents a battleground addressing our bondage to sin. Throughout His ministry, Jesus was tempted to change course and not face the Cross. He did battle with this temptation to the very end. Evil did not want the Cross to happen, and thereby see its power over humanity broken. Through the Cross, God has won our freedom from sin, death and the power of evil.

Third, the Cross represents the highest court, addressing our disobedience. Humanity stands before its Creator as a responsible creature who, in believing the lies of the evil one, has attempted to steal its existence from God. Through the costly death of His only-begotten Son upon the Cross, God has revealed that the forgiveness of sins is the deepest expression of His love and mercy.

"It is God who works in you to will and to act according to his good purpose." Philippians 2:13

A pastor was called to officiate at a graveside service for a woman from a small town. Her family was known to the pastor, and other citizens of the small community where they all lived, as quarrelsome, meddlesome, and difficult. The dead woman and her family, to put it mildly, were a wildly dysfunctional bunch. After the brief service, as the mourners were leaving the grave site, the pastor overheard one of her relatives say, "I know she is up there looking down on us." The pastor thought to himself, "Not if God has any mercy."

Speaking for myself, it gives me little comfort to think that those who have preceded me have a front row seat while our lives, with all their works and all their ways are played out on the human stage. I like to believe that in their joy, God is shielding them.

However that may be, I believe God is not only watching the errant world, He is deeply engaged, with a love that relentlessly pursues the good. In Jesus Christ we see God deeply immersed in a life committed to mercy and grace. So Paul could confidently remind the Philippian Christians that in His nearness to them and knowledge of them, God is at work, carrying out His will in Christ Jesus.

The work of brooding over the fallen world must be left to a love so deep and so enduring that it is able to look into the heart of this broken life without flinching and have the capacity and will to do something about it. In Jesus Christ we see such a love.

"The disciples came to Jesus and asked, 'Who, then, is the greatest in the kingdom of heaven?'" Matthew 18:1

What qualifies one for greatness? For some, the bar is set high. The Olympic games offer one definition as athletes compete for gold medals. Silver or bronze will not do. Winning gold equals greatness.

For others, it is fame. The bar is set low. Our celebrity-mad society elevates people to positions of greatness for no other reason than that they appear regularly on television and movie screens or have their music distributed widely.

For others, wealth is the key qualification. I have seen otherwise normal, self-respecting people descend into servile flattery, hanging on someone's every word, for no other reason than that the object of their adulation has lots of money. This sets the bar about as low as it can get.

Jesus also offers a qualification for greatness. But there is a caveat. This criteria for greatness has its basis not in this world but in God's kingdom. To be great is to become like a child. 'Lowly' is the word Jesus uses.

The kingdom's greatness is not seen in its capacity to give access to wealth and comfort. Nor does it take pride in glory and fame. The kingdom's greatness is made known in simplicity of faith, genuine cheerfulness, a lack of self-pity and bitterness, affection for people, and devotion to their well-being.

I am thankful for the lowly, childlike ones whose greatness honors the kingdom of God. I have known but a few, and do not count myself among them. I am also thankful that my falling short of the kingdom's greatness does not disqualify me from receiving its benefits. For it was upon the Coss that our Lord Jesus Christ revealed the true depths of the kingdom's greatness when in lowliness and humility He gave Himself for sinners.

"Jesus wept." John 11:35

Once there was a man who lived alone and never cried, although he had plenty to cry about. His life had been hard with much disappointment and bitter loss. He became stoic and cynical. He kept everything inside. He had given up on feeling much of anything. Really, he had given up on life. He traveled a lot on business, and one night, while resting in his hotel room, he picked up the Gideon Bible that was on the nightstand. It opened to John 11:35. He read those two words: "Jesus wept." They were the only words he saw on the page. They pursued him, opened him up with light and fire. He started crying. He could not stop. He cried and cried until, sobbing fitfully, he had cried himself to sleep. He slept long and hard and when he awoke the next morning, some things that had been with him for as long as he could remember were gone. Something new had come. It was as if he had been dead and was now alive. He knew he was not alone.

"Jesus wept." That is the shortest verse in the Bible. It means that God has arranged things in such a way that it is the easiest verse to remember. It also makes it the easiest thing to remember about Jesus.

If Jesus wept, then He knows loss and heartache, emptiness and loneliness.

If Jesus wept, then no one falls unnoticed into the abyss of death.

If Jesus wept, then God is more personal, more intimate than we can ever imagine.

If Jesus wept, then "Father forgive them..." is not a theological abstraction but a word spoken from deep sorrow by "a man of sorrows, acquainted with grief."

If Jesus wept, then He can fall in a tear, any tear, and that means your tear, anywhere, anytime.

"For we do not have a high priest who cannot sympathize with our weaknesses, but One who has been tempted in all things as we are, yet without sin." Hebrews 4:15

Red-letter New Testaments used to be very popular. The are still around. Maybe you have one or know someone who does. They highlight what Jesus said. I have never seen a New Testament that highlights what Jesus did or who He was. Is what Jesus said more important that what He did? Are His parables and stories more important than His miracles? Why all the red ink for His words when He was at least as famous for what He did and who He was? Should publishing houses print Bibles with what He did in red? How would they highlight who He was?

Those who are caught in all sorts of discontinuity highlight words in red. Words are more manageable. We resolve the wholism of Christ into a collection of wisdom sayings, accessible to and subject to our reason. We make Him into some kind of sage who dispenses proverbial tips for living, points to mull over as we stumble along, disassociated from ourselves, so far beyond the wholism of innocence that we can hardly bear it. In fact, we cannot.

Jesus words and works were one and that is the key to who He was and who He is. When word and action, wisdom and miracle, thought and spirit are completely whole, when they are perfect in purpose, there can only be one explanation: divinity is present. This is what the New Testament, in the totality of its witness, is revealing about Jesus.

Faith restores us to the trust that takes in everything at once, that receives God all at once. There is, after all, only one Living Word. In water and promise, bread and wine, in the gift of creation, we know Him like a child knows her mother's milk before speech, before abstraction, because faith restores the capacity to receive without dissembling, without dividing down.

Therefore, Jesus' words and works are one. For in their sum you may confidently see Him for who He is: God's indivisible word of grace and forgiveness given for you.

"Do you not know that all of us who have been baptized into Christ Jesus have been baptized into His death? Therefore we have been buried with Him through baptism into death, so that as Christ was raised from the dead through the glory of the Father, so we too might walk in newness of life." Romans 6:3-5

Have you ever noticed that the Bible has storm stories, wind and water stories? They appear at crucial moments. The image of the storm represents the powers that are too much for us. Each of these stories also carries a word of promise. Seen in one way, they are a catechism of Baptism.

Noah, his family and their cargo, huddle together as the wind and water pounded the ark. What does this mean for us? God promises to be our sanctuary.

Moses and the people, fleeing before the terrible vengeance of pharaoh, watched as the wind held back the water and God made a way for them.

Jesus, asleep in a boat as a stormed raged around Him, was awakened by the panic of his followers. All it took was a word from The Word and the wind and water obeyed.

What does this mean for us? God promises to meet our fear with the solid assurance of His Word.

In Baptism the wind of the Spirit combines with the water to take hold of us in such a way that we are continually brought out of death to life. In every storm, God promises to be our sanctuary, our deliverance, and to keep us, through faith, in the strong grip of His Word, "...so we, too, might walk in newness of life."

"All this is from God, who through Christ reconciled us to Himself."
2 Corinthians 5:18

Paul writes here of reconciliation, a new relationship bringing together God and humanity in Jesus Christ. We do not earn this reconciliation. The will cannot will it into being. We do not prove we are worthy of it nor can we keep it by our own strength. This new relationship with God is built upon a foundation far more enduring than anything we can offer.

Being reconciled, we are not only summoned to be different people. That is not good enough. We are killed and made alive. We are recreated. We are new creatures. God has brought something new, which is at work in us to conquer the powers of sin, death and evil. The center of this wonderful, reconciling miracle is God Himself in Jesus Christ, crucified and risen.

In Baptism, God claims us, adopts us, makes us His own. The reconciliation is God's gift, given out of His great love. We are saved by His grace through faith. In Christ, God came to us, died for us, and was raised for us. He gives us the Holy Spirit, drawing us to Himself through Word and Sacrament. He clears away the debris of our past continually opening for us a reconciled future. One day, He will complete the work of salvation and usher us into the eternal kingdom.

"All this is from God", for which we are duty bound to "thank, praise, serve and obey Him."

"The younger son got together all he had, and set off for a far country." Luke 15:13

Two young men became police officers. After a time, a friend of one of the families inquired after their son. "Oh he is doing very well," his mother reported. "He has received two promotions and is making good money. His hours are good and everyone seems to like him."

At about the same time, the other young man was fired from the same department. He had received no raises and no promotions. When his parents heard the news, they were quite upset until they learned that he had lost his job because he would not participate in the corruption that was the standard in the department.

The first young man "succeeded" according to the standards he was willing to abide by. The second young man "failed'"for the same reason.

In a real sense, it would not have mattered if the prodigal son had failed or succeeded in the far country. Either way, his life was measured by the standards of that place. Success would have been just as damning as was his groveling with the whores and pigs.

You and I were created for the standards of the Father's house. No matter how high we may fly by any others, they are not sufficient measures by which we can claim success.

In Jesus Christ, God calls us all His sons and daughters to return from the far country to the Father's house. The shape of our lives, whether rich or poor, is immaterial. What matters is that we know we are His. The Church has been given the Gospel for just this purpose. For it is through its' gracious message that we are awakened to the standards of the Kingdom and drawn into the forgiving, loving arms of the Father.

"And in Jesus Christ, His only Son, our Lord"

The section of the Apostle's Creed dealing with Jesus Christ is as significant for what it does not say as it is for what it does say. Missing from this section of the Creed is any reference to the teachings and miracles of Jesus. The language moves from His birth immediately to His death, resurrection and the events following, including His Ascension to the Father. This pattern is present in all the ancient creeds of the Church. Therefore, it is not accidental.

What is mentioned was of the greatest significance to the early Church. The details of the Christological section of the Creed provide the basis and criterion for understanding and confessing what is essential about Jesus and His Gospel.

In this article of the Creed, "crucified" appears with the words "suffered," "died" and "buried". One would think a reference to crucifixion would be superfluous under the circumstances. Why this specific reference to the manner of Jesus' death?

The answer, I believe, lies in the fact that the event of the Cross is the key to understanding the meaning of Jesus entire mission to this world. On the Cross, humanity looked upon the One who had encountered them in love and righteousness and dealt with Him as a common criminal. The event of the Cross, then, exposes human antipathy toward the Living God and puts the lie to all our claims to love justice.

The event of the crucifixion is mentioned in the Creed because this event, unlike any other in all of history, confronts men and women with the enormity of our crime; the theft of our existence and contempt for the Living God. At the same time, the Cross reveals God's intention to have mercy on us. The Cross of Jesus is the consequence of God's love, for upon it hung the One who for our need His life did give.

"Born of the virgin Mary"

There is hardly a teaching of the Church more inaccessible to modern reason than the virgin birth. The problem is simple. Conception and birth are a process of natural life which bring a person into existence who had no prior existence. Yet the Church confesses that the Son was born of Mary and has existed eternally just as God is eternal.

Faith may confess this article of the Creed with assurance, but it does not remove the stumbling block. But if the task of proclaiming the faith is to make the Son of God accessible to the world, then some way through the obstacle of our reason must be found.

Some would argue that these stories are nothing but reflections of the mythic traditions of the Hellenistic world. But this interpretation does not do justice to the forward looking character of the revelation in Christ which is anything but a falling back into myth. The infancy narratives which are contained in Matthew and Luke are subject to the revelation of Jesus Christ as the living Word of God. In Jesus, something entirely new has happened. The restraint of the birth narratives makes no room for the details of conception or the actual birth. What matters to the gospel writers is that God has revealed Himself in the flesh. Jesus' birth was as real a birth as yours or mine. At the same time, what can be said of this human birth cannot be said of any other human birth. For in Jesus God is creating a new humanity.

Therefore, the Church cannot acquiesce to the insistence of reason that the virgin birth be dismissed from our confession. For our confession preserves the mystery of the Word made flesh, in all lowliness, meekness and humility. The confession of the virgin birth, which includes the poor, lowly girl who gladly embraced God's will for her, guards against the pride of reason which refuses to receive the essential message of the Incarnation: God's salvation comes, and is willed by God, in the form of lowliness and weakness without any kind of pride, to be received in faith.

**'Pride goes before destruction, and a haughty spirit before a fall.'
Proverbs 16:18**

The Lutheran Church has come down very hard on the fact that the will of man cannot produce a pure act, a pure choice. But we have not been equally as firm on whether the mind can produce a pure thought, or proposition, or expression of the truth. We have been quick to point out that to say I have done a pure act is a form of pride. We have not been quite as willing to apply the same conclusion to those who claim to produce a pure proposition or statement of truth. Yet, this claim can also be a reflection of pride. It has gotten the Church into all kinds of trouble and continues to do so.

In the late nineteenth century, for example, the Norwegian Lutheran tradition was torn apart by what was called the 'Election Controversy.' One group emphasized the sovereignty of God. Another group focused on human responsibility. Both sides stubbornly insisted on the truth of their position. It was not until 1917 that the rift was healed, but only in part. Statements by both groups were approved. Although each one canceled out the other, the Church decided to live with both positions. This is but one example of numerous Church conflicts that reflect the consequences of the pride of the mind, of thought, of reason.

The Biblical view of man and woman is that of a creature that has been heavily compromised by sin. It is not only our actions that reflect this (and they are clear enough) but also our minds (this tends to be less clear). But pride, whatever form it takes, always has destructive, divisive consequences.

Churches continue to hold doggedly to propositions of truth to such an extent that other churches are held at arm's length, or are shut out altogether. I confess, this is something I struggle with. At the same time, I wonder: "Are the truths we confess best held in the proud battlements of the mind or in the humble synthesis of faith and love?"

**"And there is salvation in no one else, for there is no other name under heaven given among men by which we must be saved.'
Acts 4:12**

Tolerance is an important word in our culture. In a "live and let live" society such as ours a certain amount of tolerance is expected and necessary. But tolerance is not the same as indifference. A person may appear to be tolerant simply because he or she carries no convictions. This is not tolerance. Is it also a part of us?

Christians dare not worship at the cultural altar of tolerance if it leads to this bland indifference. The Christian cannot be neutral or indifferent about belief, not without denying the Lord of the Church. This we cannot tolerate. For the fact is that when we have been grasped by the Gospel of Christ, we will not be indifferent about the matter of beliefs.

Jesus calls you to be vigilant about beliefs, for there is "one name by which we are saved." Belief in Jesus is the path God has laid down by which human beings come to authentic faith. We believe and confess that in Jesus Christ all truth, meaning and purpose are revealed – for all. This is not a popular idea, nor has it ever been, as the blood of the martyrs will attest. God may have other avenues by which people are saved. We do not know. What we do know is that our Lord, in viewing the human landscape has said, "Go into all the world and make disciples of all nations, baptizing and teaching them to observe all that I have commanded you." This is not a formula for tolerance as our culture defines it, to be sure. It is something much better.

These words resonate from the heart of God, who in His love and grace has provided the way of authentic trust and belief through Jesus. When the life-changing truth of the Gospel of this same Jesus Christ is openly and courageously shared, people are freed from false belief and no belief. Their lives are set on the hopeful course of a living faith. Someone you know needs to hear this life-changing message. May God grant us the grace and courage to care less about the bland tolerance advocated by the culture and more about the all-inclusive truth that God has revealed in Jesus Christ!

"Therefore, if anyone is in Christ, he is a new creation; the old has gone, the new has come!" 2 Corinthians 5:17

If the 60's generation had an anthem it was 'Woodstock' written by Joni Mitchell. The song is about the famous rock concert, and was made popular by Crosby, Stills, Nash, and Young. The key lyric in the song is, "and we've got to get ourselves back to the garden." The garden Joni Mitchell's lyric symbolically refers to is the Garden of Eden. Woodstock was supposed to represent that return. The naive optimism of her generation hoped to realize a kind of utopian world of peace and love. Far from being the repristination of the Garden, however, Woodstock turned out to be a giant drug-fueled, rain-soaked mud bath. The Garden ended up being acres of land strewn with garbage- and shattered illusions.

The story of Adam and Eve and the Garden of Eden, which many dismiss as primitive and quaint, is an accurate and profound picture of humanity. The story tells us that we were created for God, for creation and for one another. We were created to take our greatest delight and joy in God, to live within the luxuriant abundance of creation and be lost in love for one another. The story goes on to reveal that a tragic break in all these relationships has resulted in the world as we know it. Now, we are estranged creatures - estranged from God, from the creation and from one another. The fact that Adam and Eve hid from God served to reveal that self-consciousness now dominated them. When one of their two sons went on to murder the other, the trajectory of the ascendant self was seen to be the inheritance of fallen man and woman.

We will not "get ourselves back to the garden." Innocence is no longer possible for us. But God has promised a new creation. In Jesus Christ that new creation has begun. In God's time, this old discordant creation will give way to the new. In the meantime, faith in God's promises tempers the self so that the restoration may begin; that we may love one another, care for the world and find our deepest joy in God Himself even as we look forward, in faith and hope, to the final restoration of all things in Christ.

"Why was this ointment not sold for three hundred denarii and given to the poor?" John 12:5

It was not Jesus who said this, it was Judas. As far as he was concerned, pouring expensive ointment on the feet of Jesus was a waste. Better to sell it and distribute the cash. Judas had no time for 'Divine Wastefulness.'

There is a lot of waste and redundancy in nature. Many plants, for example, toss off bushels of seeds, most of which never take root and grow. Why has God created such a wasteful natural economy? Couldn't we have gotten by with fewer snowflakes, flowers, mountains, or lakes? Didn't God go a bit far in creating such a luxurious world?

A man who was raised during the Great Depression once observed that his family saved everything from bits of string to used nails and old boards. In later years, after the Depression had lifted, he continued to save nearly everything. He spent money on only the necessities and was critical of anyone who spent in excess, as he understood it. He allowed his experience of want to overshadow his abundance.

Surely, God expects us to use good stewardship and wisdom when we spend money, even for the church. But there is also such a thing as thinking we are economizing when we are simply being stingy.

God has gone over the top in providing for us; an abundant world points to an even more abundant grace. Many set the parameters of their generosity based on the shifting tides of the world's economies. The woman who poured expensive ointment on Jesus' feet set the course for Christian gratitude by looking to the economy of 'Divine Wastefulness' and the extravagance of God's amazing grace, revealed supremely in Jesus Christ.

"Give diligence to present yourself approved by God, a workman who doesn't need to be ashamed, properly handling the Word of Truth." 2 Timothy 2:15

Properly handling the many ways words are used is among the greatest of human responsibilities. And among these, none is more important, more crucial, than the proper handling of God's Word. For many Christians, the right tool for the proper handling of God's Word is learning to distinguish between Law and Gospel.

Law words handle God's concern for justice, righteousness, holiness. Jesus used law words. Sometimes God has to use them on you. Law words say things like, "No more games. No more lies. No more nonsense. Stop! Turn around! Knock it off!" Law words confront us with the fact that innocence is no longer possible. Law words rightly judge us and show us our need for a Savior. Sometimes, taking care of God's Word means using law words.

Gospel words are the other side of law words, like a coin. Gospel words properly handle the forgiveness of sins. Jesus called them 'keys.' Their job of gospel words is to open. Gospel words give access, permission, promise, freedom. Gospel words say things like,"Your sins are forgiven. Yes, you may. You are loved. Grace is for you, too. This is my body and blood, for you. God works everything for good. Christ Jesus will raise you from the dead." Gospel words give us the Savior we need.

When the Church struggles with itself over which words to use as we seek to properly handle the faith, this should neither surprise or dismay us. After all, if a surgeon takes care to use the right instrument in order to 'properly handle' a critical procedure, and if a master carpenter makes the effort to ensure that his blades are properly sharpened before carving the wood, how much more ought the people of God be attentive to the proper handling of the Word of God?

"Faith comes by hearing, and hearing by the Word of Christ."
Romans 10:17

My library, divided between my home and church studies, is full of books. They cover a wide range of topics. But there is one book that towers above them all. That book is the Bible.

Like other books, you can cast your line into the pages of the Bible and pull out wisdom, poetry, history, letters, stories and other forms and types of literature. The knowledge and information gathered there can be enlightening and informative. At the same time, if knowledge and information is all you take from the Bible, in a very real sense, it has fallen short of its purpose. For unlike other books, the Bible is an instrument of revelation. Through the Bible, God catches you!

The history of the Church long before the Protestant Reformation, is filled with the stories of those who were gripped by God's grace through an encounter with the Bible. The written page became the sacred page. In this respect, Martin Luther took up a lens that had been in use for centuries and adjusted its focus.

At the center of the Biblical story is Jesus Christ, the Living Word of God. This fact reveals to us that God is a wordsmith, using the symbols and sounds of language to forge faith in the hearts of those who hear His voice. This is why Saint Paul could say, "Faith comes by hearing, and hearing by the Word of Christ." When you pick up the Bible, explosive potential is in your hands. Read expectantly, for God is seeking you through the words given there.

"There are also many other things which Jesus did; were every one of them to be written, I suppose that the world itself could not contain the books." John 21:25

Books and paintings always want to go to how it was before the book was written and before the color was applied to canvas. Books and paintings reflect stories.

This is how we hear the gospel writers. Before anything was ever written, something happened. The gospel writers did not set out to write theology, expecting dispassionate academics to parse out every jot and tittle ad nauseum. They wrote of what they had seen and heard. They had a story to tell. A story that was written upon their experience and the experience of others, with Jesus. They told the story before they wrote the story. What do you do with something when you know it and want to make it known?

So much more was said. So much more happened - to them, for them. Worlds of books could not report it all. How utterly inadequate writing it down must have seemed. John says as much. His life was so full of Jesus, he could not imagine a world big enough to contain all that could be said. What a picture John was imagining: books filling valleys, tumbling over mountain ranges, filling oceans, smothering continents. Books piled so high they reach like skyscrapers into the clouds and beyond; a vast, library of grace consumed with a single, glorious theme: "the old, old, story of Jesus and His love." It is a story mighty enough to consume worlds, and tender enough to fill your heart.

"From the same mouth come blessing and cursing. My brethren, this ought not to be so." James 3:10

During the Revolutionary War, General George Washington issued an order condemning the widespread use of profanity among the soldiers of the American army. He urged his officers, by example and influence, to address the problem, observing that such speech is an insult and impiety before heaven.

Today, many would scoff at such a concern. The use of profanity is cool, chic, and worldly. The expression, "Oh my God," for example, has become as common as dirt. Many use the name of Jesus Christ in the same breath with words I will not use here.

The tongue is the mightiest weapon, even in a day of nuclear bombs and other weaponry of unimaginable power. With the ungodly tongue, dictators fan the embers of hate into flames of war. With the ungodly tongue, the sensitivities and intimacies of human sexuality are regularly cheapened. Ungodly men and women use the power of speech against the very God who gave them that power, and one another.

This week, in your congregation, you will join with others in songs of praise and prayers of thanksgiving, the language, and speech of worship. One person called this our "Sunday speech." We choose our words carefully so that our "Sunday speech" might honor the One in whose name we gather, who has given us life, by whose Cross we have been redeemed, into whose name we have been Baptized. And having tuned our tongues to the sound of praise and thanksgiving, it is our prayer that our "Sunday speech" will sound in all our words, seven days a week.

"But God raised him from the dead...because it was impossible for death to keep its hold on him." Acts 2:24

The Golden Gate is located on the eastern side of the famous temple mount in Jerusalem. The current gate was erected over an earlier structure dating from the time of Jesus. According to tradition, this is where the Messiah will arrive when He comes to establish the new Jerusalem.

In 1514, the Muslim conqueror, Suleiman, had the gate sealed in an effort to prevent the Messiah from entering. For insurance, a cemetery was placed around the entrance since it was believed the Messiah would not enter a cemetery. Somehow I do not think stone walls and dead bodies are much of a deterrent. Not for the Messiah I know.

Three days after others put Him in a cemetery, in a tomb sealed with stone, God brushed the stone aside and Jesus re-entered life. In His own body, Christ Jesus gave us a sign that no barrier will hold Him and no cemetery is off limits. But Christ Jesus did not come out of that tomb as a vengeful conqueror, bent on destruction. Oh, He came out as conqueror to be sure. But it was death that lay vanquished at His feet, and the great barrier of sin no longer stood between humanity and God.

Suleiman had no clue who he was dealing with where our Messiah is concerned. Christ Jesus will break down every dividing wall, empty every cemetery, and on that great and glorious day, establish the New Jerusalem - with gates wide open - where all the promises of God will find their fulfillment in Him.

**"Though I walk in the midst of trouble, you preserve my life."
Psalm 138:7**

Helmut Thielicke was an eminent pastor and theologian who served a congregation in Stuttgart, Germany during the devastating days of World War II. Pastor Thielicke lived through the worst of the war along with his congregation. None of the magnitude of the suffering was lost on him. Harassment and numerous interrogations by the Gestapo also took a toll. But through all of it, he was able to help others to recognize what it meant to be in the gracious grip of God, even when the cruel grip of man seemed inescapable and absolute. And he was able to do so because he knew that Jesus also stood in that place.

Jesus faced gross injustice, was battered and brutalized at the hands of man. Like you and me, His sufferings also drove Him to look into the heavens. And he did so from the apparent godlessness of the bloody cross. But Jesus threw up no litany of anger, self-pity or blame. Three words he uttered there gave testimony to the whole of His life. These three words can give direction to our laments when life seems too much, when God seems to distant, even absent, when events overwhelm, "Into Your hands."

"Why does your Teacher eat with tax collectors and sinners?"
Matthew 9:11

John, a widower, lived next door to Robert, also a widower, whose wife had recently died. Robert's relatives lived far away and could rarely get away to visit. For his part, Robert was too frail to travel. He longed for friends, for companionship, but his off-putting, quirky personality made him hard to like. John avoided Robert at every opportunity, finding excuses to turn down invitations to visit, never going outside if his neighbor was in the yard. John was fully aware of Robert's loneliness, yet he withheld the gift of friendship. Then, one Sunday morning, as he arrived home from church, John saw an ambulance parked on the street in front of Robert's house. A few moments later, a stretcher was wheeled down the sidewalk next door. Robert's body was covered with a sheet. He had committed suicide.

The sins of commission are frightening enough; the things we willfully do, knowing they are wrong. But the sins of omission can be terrifying in the extreme, if we have any sensitivity. These are the things we ought to have done that we leave undone. There is no end to the rationalizations we can call up in our defense. Either our lives are too full of obligations to be bothered with others, or we decide the neighbor is undeserving of our help.

Jesus got Himself into all kinds of trouble because He went out of His way to be there for those who others found plenty of reason to avoid. He took up the obligation to care for the neighbor not because they were lovable or likable, but because the need was there and love could do no other.

Are you and I so attractive, lovable and likable that God simply could not resist us and therefore, gave us His only begotten Son to die for us? Hardly. If we dare to claim, to our benefit, His grace, mercy, love and forgiveness, by what rationale do we dare withhold from one another the benefit of a neighbor's concern?

"...and let us consider how to stimulate one another to love and good deeds, not forsaking our own assembling together, as is the habit of some, but encouraging one another..." Hebrews 10:24-25

We gathered as strangers from various countries. Labor was divided, we each knew our task. Our chef guided us along the way. In the midst of the laughter, joking, the sounds of chopping, mixing, the clanging of pots and pans and much lively conversation, a bond began to form among us. After a few hours, our various efforts resulted in the fulfillment of our common purpose. Dinner was served.

This describes a cooking class Linda and I attended in Siena, Italy. It's also not a bad picture of what a congregation can look like: people called together to engage their life's energies and resources with a common purpose.

Sadly, many church kitchens are virtually empty when it comes to the preparations for ministry. Life's energies and resources are invested elsewhere. Many are happy to sit down at the table and receive the meal, but moving into the kitchen to assist in the preparations is another matter.

Wherever you may be as you read this, if you are a part of a Christian community, that community is the place where God has placed you to share in the exploration and preparation of ministry. The nourishing, simple fare of Word and sacrament is the main course. That never changes. It is always there for you. At the same time, the many and various possibilities for expanding the feast of love and service are endless. But there is more to it than that. Engaging in active ministry with others widens and strengthens the bonds of fellowship, sets an example for children, provides a witness to family, friends, business associates and neighbors, develops leadership, and multiplies the joy that comes with working and serving together for the greater purposes of God's Kingdom.

So, what are you waiting for? Grab your apron and head for the kitchen. You'll be glad you did! Ciao!

"He went away sorrowful, for he had many possessions." Matthew 19:22

Just when you thought you had finally gotten ahold of the big thing, the next big thing comes along. Neighbors cast a wary, envious glance at the new car in the driveway next door, the fear of inadequacy sets in and the planning for an even better car begins. You get the picture. You may be in it.

Fear may lie at the heart of our insatiable need to acquire. Fear of what other people think of us, fear of the future and our need to hedge ourselves against its uncertainties, fear of that emptiness into which many pour possessions and experiences, as if filling a void. But it does not work. Take a good, long look at those you envy, those who reach the pinnacles of financial and material comfort. They imprison themselves within gated communities, squadrons of security guards, compounds and estates, fearing the loss of possessions, person and privacy. Self-reliance does nothing to eradicate fear. Fear simply changes its form.

We all know the story. A wealthy young man asked Jesus what it would take to have eternal life. Jesus' answer was short, simple, and terrifying: " Sell what you have and give the money to the poor, and follow me." The man walked away from Jesus, full of sorrow. The fear of loss, of giving up what he possessed, paralyzed him with grief.

The meaning in Jesus story is clear: what we pride ourselves on, our self-reliance, is actually the great sin of unbelief - and that includes certain forms of free-will Christianity which is nothing more than self-reliance gone to church. For unbelief is not the refusal to give assent to certain doctrines, catechisms or Biblical truths. Unbelief is nothing more than the refusal to count on God, to trust Him.

Confidence rooted in self-reliance, religious or otherwise, never shakes the fear that our efforts and willing may not deliver the goods. Confidence rooted in God's promises results in a faith which moves with assurance through the day into God's promised future, whether God delivers the goods or not. For reliance on God means reliance on His will, and not our own.

"What is the price of two sparrows--one copper coin? But not a single sparrow can fall to the ground without your Father knowing it...So don't be afraid; you are worth more than many sparrows."
Matthew 10:29

Linda and I stepped into a Honk Kong eatery and were seated at large, round table. Next to me was a young man reading the morning paper. His name was Feng, a computer programmer from Beijing who spoke good English. Feng ordered a sampling of dishes for us, assuring us we would be pleased (we were), and for a few minutes we enjoyed friendly conversation in what had been a room full of strangers.

You don't have to travel far from home to find yourself in the nameless crowd. We pass by strangers every day. They give us no thought. We give no thought to them. I am always amazed at how people can stand in line at the grocery store, for example, within a foot or two of someone, and not have anything to say. This numbing indifference to others, in which we are all implicated, is part of living in a fearful world estranged from its Creator. It takes its toll on all of us.

A man once told me he hated to be in crowds. This was not because he suffered from agoraphobia, but because he felt more alone in a crowd than anywhere else. He is not alone. Not being noticed is a burden that many carry, even in the midst of the most intimate relationships.

To hear that God's knowledge of me is intimate and total would be too much to bear were it not for Jesus. For the One who presses upon us the promise of His fearful nearness, is the same One who gave His life for us, who comes near in mercy, forgiveness and love in His Word and the sacraments. Jesus gave the promise in the verse above to His disciples as He prepared to send them into a hostile world. He wanted them to know that they would always be in the Father's eye, on His mind, and in His heart. He wants you to know that too.

"Train a child in the way he should go..." Psalm 22:6

I attended my first opera when I was eight years old. The place was Honolulu, where my father served as an Air Force chaplain. The occasion was the opening night of Verdi's 'Aida,' a dramatic story set in ancient Egypt. The role of the pharaoh was sung by my father. The sounds and images of that night seemed to transport me to the banks of the Nile. I remember it like it was yesterday.

In the years that followed, I developed a growing interest in ancient Egypt and read everything I could find. By the time college came around, I majored in ancient history and gave serious thought to studying archaeology with the goal of digging in the sands of Egypt. The call to ministry set another course, but my interest in Egypt has never faded. My dad and mom could not have predicted that one night at the opera would nearly result in a vocation as an egyptologist. An opera lover, maybe. But an egyptologist?

As Christian parents we can never predict with any certainty how our lives may influence our children. But this much is certain: influence them we will. And when Christian worship, learning, witness and service are the shaping and defining pattern of their parents' lives, we can know that these influences can only help to define and shape our children as they come to know and trust in the God who loves them in Jesus Christ.

"I do not understand my own actions. For I do not do what I want, but I do the very thing I hate." Romans 7:15

The language Saint Paul uses here describes the gap between what someone once called, "The is and the ought." Paul writes from that gap. It is where we all find ourselves. But how do we deal with it?

Some ignore the gap and resolve themselves into their desires and impulses, letting what is simply be what is. In the 1960's they put it this way, "If it feels good, do it."

Others are driven by the gap to take a higher road and recognize that some form of ethical and moral effort are necessary. The struggle to be fully human must progress beyond the level of animal impulse.

Humor is another response. Laughing at the gap is sometimes the best that we can do.

Then there are those who are consumed by the gap, those for whom the tensions between what is and what ought to be are too much. They fall into despair, cynicism, even madness.

Whatever approach we take to the gap, ignoring it, battling it, laughing at it or allowing it to overwhelm, the outcome remains the same. The gap is never closed. We remain caught in the tension between "the is and the ought."

It is surprising, then, to know that even as he laments life in the gap, Paul does so as one for whom the gap has been closed! The yawning chasm between his humanity and its fulfillment was crossed at the Cross. Only the forgiveness of God in Christ is strong enough, enduring enough to close the gap between what we are and what we ought to be.

We are not yet what we will be, and we share this burden with the apostle. But we do not sing in a minor key. Even our laments ring with joyous hope as we look forward to that Day when the gap between "the is and the ought" will, in every way be closed and God's great work of reconciliation in Jesus Christ will be complete.

"And early in the morning, while it was still dark, He arose and went out and departed to a lonely place, and was praying there."
Mark 1:35

Linda and I settled in at Tenaya Lodge, just a few miles outside of Yosemite National Park. It is quiet there. The atmosphere invites solitude, rest and reflection, dimensions of living that can be hard to come by.

Several years ago we spent part of a day in another quiet place, the Sea of Galilee. It looks much as it did when Jesus and His disciples lived along its quiet shores. And it is not hard to understand why the Lord made that remote, tranquil place His home, His resting point.

The life of faith is lived in a world of conflict, tension and struggle, much of which militates against the faith itself. Our Lord knew that battle, and those who belong to Him know it too. So, at regular intervals, Jesus withdrew to places of solitude where prayer and rest were His only work.

Disconnecting from daily life does not require a long trip to a remote place. We can all find space and quiet places that are near at hand. A few moments with the Scriptures, in quiet contemplation, can center us again in God's promises, clear the clutter from our distracted lives and refresh us in that peace that world neither knows nor can give.

"There is neither Jew nor Gentile, neither slave nor free, nor is there male and female, for you are all one in Christ Jesus." Galatians 3:28

A visit to Rome must include the famous Pantheon. As its name suggests, it was most likely a temple that celebrated all the gods. Visitors from all over the Roman empire would find in this great edifice reason to celebrate their diversity.

Our culture calls upon us to celebrate diversity and has embraced this idea to the point of making it a virtual absolute. No culture, idea, tradition, aesthetic, etc, is of more value than any other, except the idea of diversity, of course. One definition of celebrate is, "to praise widely." If that is what the culture wants me to do on behalf of diversity, I am not so sure.

The trumpeting of the glories of diversity by the culture is not surprising. The culture is really at a stand-off here. They really have nowhere else to go. But is cultural window shopping the best we can do? What, if anything, is capable of actually moving beyond the stalemate of diversity into unity? For that is something I would want to praise widely.

Saint Paul points us beyond a world defined by relative distinctions to a world defined by its relationship to God in Christ. Jew, Greek, slave, free, male and female are not ultimate categories. What is of ultimate importance is that they have all been caught up in the great, unifying power of God's love and grace in Jesus Christ.

For the Christian, the great unifying reality in life is not the principle of diversity. We celebrate, in the truest sense of the word, the unity we know in Jesus Christ. I will tolerate diversity, but it is not something I will celebrate. I will save that for Jesus, in whose glorious name diverse peoples of every race and nation are reconciled in the authentic unity of God's gracious love.

"Whatever is true, whatever is honorable, whatever is just, whatever is pure, whatever is lovely, whatever is gracious, if there is any excellence, if there is anything worthy of praise, think about these things." Philippians 4:8

Where do such words find a voice today? Certainly not in the cultural chorus of jaded cynicism which mocks just about everything on Paul's list. After all, worldliness is chic, hip. Vulgarity is cool. Paul's list of terms belongs to a world of Pollyannas and fifties sitcoms. We all know that in the "real world" there is no room for the language of innocence. Right?

Wrong. The "real world" is an expression which actually describes the fallen, unreal world where innocence is not at home and the most intimate of fellowships is the fellowship of sin. In that world, the language works like this:

"Whatever is false, whatever is dishonorable, whatever is unjust, whatever is ugly, whatever is merciless, if there is anything debased, if there anything worthy of ridicule, think about these things."

Paul knew that the freedom won for us in Christ Jesus restores a kind of innocence to living, to our thoughts, words and actions. Faith gives expression to that freedom: the freedom to love as we have been loved, the freedom to affirm, enjoy and reflect with gratitude on what is good in life, the freedom to look ahead in confident hope to the restoration of the real world, where God's children will live in innocence, righteousness, and blessedness forever.

"Go, and do likewise." Luke 10:37

Are you a good, law abiding citizen? You would probably say so. The police do not show up at your front door, your taxes get paid and you manage to find the voting booth. Oh, you might exceed the speed limit now and then or grouse about the neighbors but who doesn't? All in all, you manage to stay within the confines of legality and are no threat to law and order.

When it comes to the law, most of us play defense. We stay safely behind the prescribed fences, not unlike those who walked by the poor fellow in the parable of the Good Samaritan. He had been badly beaten and left for dead. The two men who passed him by did so for perfectly acceptable legal reasons. No one would have faulted them. To have touched this man would have made them ritually unclean.

In pressing His point, Jesus tells His disciples that a Samaritan (the Jews and Samaritans hated each other) was also passing by, saw the injured man and had compassion on him. Jesus then asked, "Which of these three was a neighbor to the man that fell among the robbers? The one who had mercy on him. Go, and do likewise."

The Samaritan did not keep the law, he fulfilled the law. The difference is huge. Those who seek to fulfill the law play offense, not defense. They actively seek the welfare, the good of the neighbor. They live way beyond the law in the realm of love, the realm of mercy, without any pride, where there is nothing to fear. All of a sudden, being a law abiding citizen does not have quite the same ring to it, does it?

Faith in Christ brings real freedom. Christians are 'free range' lovers, wandering through the world looking for any excuse to pour love and mercy all over everything. When our Lord Jesus says, "Go, and do likewise," He is turning loose on a world of law keepers, a horde of law fulfillers created by faith. Nobody should be allowed to have this much fun!

"What does it profit a man if he should gain the whole world but lose his soul?" Mark 8:36

Hannah was already in her nineties when I became her pastor. She was home-bound so I stopped by with communion each month. Coffee was always ready and Hannah liked to remember the old days.

Just south of the small, northwestern Minnesota town where we lived, an old log cabin struggled for survival in a grove of oaks and brush. Hannah was born in that cabin and spent her childhood there.

She once told me about the Native Americans who came through the area each spring, on their way from Minnesota to the Dakotas. They would stop for a few days and set up camp in the meadow near the old cabin, visiting and trading with her father and some of the other local farmers. Her parents and their guests also shared something else, their Christian faith.

During one visit I asked her the obvious question: 'What has been the biggest change you have seen in your life-time?' I'm not sure what I expected. Maybe she would marvel at the space program, automobiles, the telephone, or running water, at the very least. What was Hannah's reply? "Not much has changed. People are still the same. God is still faithful," she said, her voice still carrying a Scandinavian edge.

I suppose I should have expected this kind of sober wisdom from a woman who grew up in a log cabin. Her life had been tuned to relationships and the Christian faith, not to things. Gaining the world was not important to her. Her soul was.

"When you do it to the least of these my brethren, you do it unto me." Matthew 25:40

A vineyard was our backyard for a couple of days during a stay in the Napa Valley. The beautiful vines stood, row after row, in military precision. They received lavish amounts of attention, and no resource was spared to ensure they produced the best possible grapes. The truth is, these vines receive better care than most people.

Of course, there are certain advantages to taking care of vines. They do not complain, talk back, or resist efforts to provide for them. Vines present certain challenges, to be sure, but they stay where they are put and generally do not exhibit annoying, unlikable personalities. Not so with people. That is not to suggest that some people are not provided for simply for what can be gained from them. But this is not caring.

To care is to have regard for the whole person, warts and all. And it is not easy, because most of our inclinations are in the direction of self-care. Over the centuries, the Church developed into an institution that could be relied upon to care for those whom it was easy to forget. Monasteries and churches became places of sanctuary where countless lives found compassion, healing and support during some very dark and brutal times.

God calls us in Jesus Christ to be a caring community. This caring can and does run in many directions, and it is not always welcome when it arrives in the neighborhood. It is good, then, to remember that our Lord's compassion and caring was not always met with gratitude. But that was not His motivation, to be thanked. He cared for others, because it is in the nature of love to do so.

Christ Jesus left His Church with a powerful image of caring that challenges the faithful of each generation. Surveying the hungry, thirsty, naked and imprisoned, He turns to us and says, in effect, "When you care for them, you care for me."

"He gives power to the faint, and to him who has no might he increases strength." Isaiah 40:27-31

I do not know if young parents today teach their kids the old nursery rhymes. My guess is most do not. If so, it's a shame. Take, for example, the old rhyme "Little Jack Horner."

'Little Jack Horner sat in a corner eating his Christmas pie. He stuck in his thumb, pulled out a plumb, and said, 'Oh, what a good boy am I.'"

I have never had Christmas pie, but I am familiar with the moral of this little ditty and its logic: Little Jack concluded that the plum was his reward for being good. Goodness is rewarded with a treat.

Ancient Israel was in a bad neighborhood. They enjoyed a very brief period of glory under David and his son Solomon. But for most of their history, they were run over by one conquering army after another. Their little country lay in the lanes of traffic as stronger countries swarmed through the region, took them into exile, and made them strangers on the earth. Why should they have had any trust, any faith, in God at all? There was no evidence to conclude they were in God's great favor. So, it is not surprising, as Isaiah recounts, that they had questions about God. But in the end, what came to characterize Israel was not doubt, but faith-faith in God's faithfulness.

A strange fact of history is that abundance and success rarely result in faith-religion, maybe, but not faith. Truth be told, Israel's faith was born out of weakness and not strength, failure, not success. When the crowds began to gather around Jesus, because he seemed to be popular, He cautioned them: "The birds have their nests, the foxes their dens, but the Son of Man has no place to lay His head." There is no security in power or might that may be drawn from following Jesus.

The Little Jacks and Jills of this world look at their abundance and congratulate themselves, sustained by the evidence of their deserving. People of faith look to the cross, seeing there the evidence of our spiritual poverty, our undeserving, and are sustained by the One whose power and grace are made perfect in weakness.

"For the Son of Man came not to be served but to serve..."
Matthew 20:28

Protestants have not made too much of Mary. But it is not hard to see why she became so prominent. Once the Church moved into the vacuum created by the fall of the Roman empire, both in the Latin west and the Greek-speaking east, the weak, suffering, despised Jesus of the cross became the all-powerful, triumphant Christ reigning over the heavens. This emphasis supported the politics of the churchmen, but it left a lot of ordinary people struggling to relate to an exalted, triumphant King Jesus. While the winners raised great marble mega-churches, symbolic of triumph, the losers had to look for someone to understand them. Mary was more down to earth, more accessible. Perhaps she would listen and then gain the ear of her exalted Son who was no longer cast in the role of the weak one, acquainted with grief.

The Church has always been tempted to celebrate the triumph of the empty tomb at the expense of the Cross. We call this tendency the 'Theology of Glory.' None of us have to be taught this theology. You have it in you from birth. Left to ourselves we want a God who fixes all the problems, makes everything work, tells me what to do. The 'Theology of Glory' is preoccupied with seeing the evidence of faith in the experiences and successes of our lives. The Theology of Glory wants churches filled with uplifting music and positive sermons that give me the keys to successful living. You probably have a good dose of this in you. You probably want to be a winner. If so, you need conversion.

Ministry does not move from strength, from power, from success. In a real sense, these things can obscure the cross and the faith itself. If you are to minister, you cannot be the strong one. If you are to minister, it cannot be about you. You may have some apparent strength that others may lean on, but if it is not also apparent that you know weakness, it is doubtful that you can minister. Someone once said, paraphrasing the Lord, "Winners want to be served. Losers want to serve. Losers make the best ministers."

"Save, Lord; we are perishing!" And he said to them, 'Why are you afraid, O men of little faith? 'Then he rose and rebuked the winds and the sea; and there was a great calm." Matthew 8:24-26

The late Alvin Rogness (former president of Luther Seminary, Saint Paul, Minnesota) once told a story from his days as a young father. He and his wife Nora had six small children. He would often lay awake at night, worrying about what would become of Nora and the kids if anything should happen to him. These anxieties burdened him and when they did, he thought back to a moment when he was six years old. His father was ill during the influenza epidemic of 1919 which killed many people. While his father lay sick in another room, Al climbed into bed with his mother. He asked her, "Mommy, what will we do if Daddy dies?" His mother replied, "God will take care of us." Then, he was able to go to sleep.

After my divorce almost thirty years ago, I took a two-year sabbatical, moved to Denver, Colorado and worked for my brother. No longer a husband, away from my sons, friends and the ministry, the role adjustments were overwhelming. Like my friend Al Rogness, I lay awake at night, filled with anxiety over the future. Then, one day a Christian co-worker, sensing my fears, took me aside. He said, "Mark, you are a pastor. Don't ever forget something you have probably said to many. God takes care of His people." Those simple words of promise opened the future for me. Fear was gone. Trust returned.

Caught in a storm, the disciples were gripped by fear. It was not that they had no faith. They had too little faith, and the Lord told them so. This is where most of us find ourselves. Perhaps you find yourself laying awake at night in these chaotic and turbulent times, hounded by fears, consumed with what might be, fearful of being overwhelmed. If so, I have a word that meets you in your greatest fears and your flimsy faith: God takes care of His people. He really does, you know. It is a promise you can trust. For it comes from Him who calms wind and sea-and fearful hearts.

The Pride of the Mind

A good friend once commented that every person who serves on a theological faculty should be mandated to teach confirmation classes and visit nursing homes as part of their job description. What does a Biblical theologian resplendent with a Ph.D. have to say to a teenager in love with ipods, laptops and pop culture? What does a high flying systematics professor have to say to a woman living out her last months in a nursing home on some nameless side street, neglected or forgotten by her family and the 'progressing' world around her?

If professional theologians have nothing to say to the teenage pop culture addict or a dying woman, then I have a hard time understanding what they have to say to a classroom full of seminarians destined for the trenches to do battle with "sin, death and the power of the devil". Naturally, many would object to this. But the course descriptions of a typical mainline seminary today, Lutheran or otherwise, reveal a simple fact: the "schools of the prophets" have become graduate schools in religion, where the religiously diverse and inclusive values of the culture have made Jesus just one more option on the religious salad bar.

Theological faculties and congregations would do well to remember that it is what the Church has to say to the fallen world, in its state of perpetual bondage and lostness unto death, that finally matters. The academic culture and the wider society, with all their generous diversity, have no answer to these. Jesus does. For Christ, and the salvation that is in Him alone, is the heart, soul and substance of the Church's message. It is in the sounding of this one, glorious note that the Church finds its voice, and the world its hope.

"For by grace you have been saved through faith; and that not of yourselves, it is the gift of God." Ephesians 2:8-9

A young man called out of the blue and wanted to talk. The next morning found him in my study, wringing his hands, full of doubt. He had been baptized and grew up in a Lutheran congregation. During his college years, a friend convinced him that his Baptism meant nothing and that he must make a free-will decision to accept Christ. The next few years found him in a so-called non-denominational church.

He went on to describe a Christian life, as it had been presented to him, that was a source of chronic uncertainty. It began with the demand that he make a free-will decision. Then, the message he heard continually prodded the will to keep choosing, setting up Biblical principles for living, ladders of spiritual achievement, rules for godly living. The questions poured out of him. Am I doing what God wants? Am I praying often enough? Am I loving enough? Do I have enough faith? Am I sincere in wanting to love God or am I just afraid of judgment? When I die will I have done enough to escape God's judgment? Am I really a sincere Christian?

After listening to his litany of questions, I replied: "I don't know you, but I can say with certainty that the answer to all your questions is no'. At the same time, I can say with even more certainty that the answer to your doubts is Christ and what He has done for you. Basing faith on your decision for Christ is a formula for uncertainty. Basing faith on Christ's decision for you in your Baptism plants you firmly in the Gospel."

What the young man who came to me was discovering is that when we look to ourselves, to what we have done, to our willing, all God will show us is our unwillingness. God deliberately drives us to uncertainty, doubt, despair or, even worse, to pride. What I hoped he would see is that when we begin with baptism, with God's decision for us, God shows us the righteousness that is His gift to us by faith, deliberately leading us away from ourselves to the foot of the Cross, to the forgiveness that flows from His merciful heart.

"I am praying for them; I am not praying for the world but for those whom you have given me, for they are yours." John 17:9

A pastor who frequently traveled on church business developed a habit. Before he checked out of a hotel room, he would pray for the next occupants of that room, that God would be with them and bless them. This is called intercessory prayer.

One of the great blessings and comforts of the Christian life is to know that others are praying for you. The knowledge of this has strengthened me and I am sure you can say the same. It is wonderful to know that intercession is being made for you in the midst of life's hurts and hopes.

It is even more wonderful to know that our Divine Friend and Brother, Jesus our Savior, is praying for us. The 17th chapter of the Gospel of John records the great intercessory prayer of Jesus. He prays for the small group of believers who are with Him. He prays that the Father may guard them against disunity, that they may be one in heart and mind. He prays that they may be shielded from evil, sanctified in the truth, and that one day they may be with Him and see His glory. But does He pray for you and me?

In verse 20 we read, "I do not pray for these only, but also for those who are to believe in me through their word." And in Hebrews 7:25 we are told that Christ Jesus "always lives to make intercession for them."

Someone once wondered how it can be that God prays to Himself. What can it mean to say that Jesus, the Second Person of the Holy Trinity, prays to the Father, and for the intercession of the Holy Spirit on our behalf? The truth is, we cannot know. Nor do we need to. It is enough to know that every detail of our lives reaches the deepest intimacies of Christ's love for us. We are on His mind and, though it is a mystery, in His prayers also.

"Show me your ways, Lord, teach me your paths. Guide me in your truth." Psalm 25:4-5

For generations, Paolo's family has been riding the waters of the Venetian lagoon, guiding gondolas through the maze of canals and waterways. Linda and I began our excursion with him at the great landing next to Saint Mark's square. It wasn't long before we were gliding along the narrow canals, in the fading light of dusk, with no idea where we were. But Paolo knew. I was reassured by his calm demeanor and steady gaze. His handling of the gondola was elegant and effortless. This was someone who knew where he was, where he was going, and how to get there.

When I look ahead at the day before me, there is reason enough to wonder about what the right direction might be. Even if I am convinced, obstacles, threats and dangers may cause me to question my course. When I look at the wider world, I have even less reason for confidence. There appears to be no real direction in life. The course seems to be one of random chaos and confusion.

If the Bible makes anything clear it is that the hand of God is on the tiller of history. The voyage is not without tumult and danger, to be sure. But the direction is set and the course, however torturous, will end in the fulfillment of God's good and gracious purposes. Knowing this helps me step back a bit and remember that I am not wandering blindly through life, in the hands of chaotic forces.

In your Baptism, God gave you the Holy Spirit, to be your Comforter and Guide. If an earthly guide, like our friend Paolo, can navigate so adroitly, how much more is the Spirit of Christ, Who is the Way, the Truth, and the Life, able to guide us through the convolutions and perils of living?

"Speaking the truth in love..." Ephesians 4:15

I have read books that contain voluminous footnotes. On occasion, you can become so engrossed in them that the momentum shifts to these parenthetical matters and you can lose focus.

This reminds me of the seminary intern who had a disagreement with his supervising pastor over Biblical authority. The intern was assigned to preach on the Gospel text for the day, John 3:16, the verse that Martin Luther once called "the Gospel in miniature." He read the text and then concluded, "So says the Bible. The Bible is true and you can know the Bible is true for the following ten reasons." He was off to the races on his "ten reasons", in a stubborn defense of his view of the Bible, and left the text in the dust. An important footnote displaced the even more important central theme.

One way to trace the history of the Church is to trace this pattern of parenthetical matters demanding to be the center of attention. In recent decades the Lutheran church, of which I am a member, has been torn apart by the tensions resulting from this dynamic.

During the decade of the 1970's, the Lutherans were at war over the question of Biblical authority.

In the 1980's, concern over dwindling church attendance led to conflict between traditionalists and those who were marketing the Church like some new breakfast cereal.

Beginning in the late 1990's, insistence on the adoption of a form of the historic episcopacy led to widespread protests within the Evangelical Lutheran Church in America. This bitter conflict has produced numerous opposition groups and one entirely new Lutheran denomination.

These matters (and many more that could be mentioned) are legitimate subjects, worthy of the application of our concern as Christians. To say something is parenthetical is not to say it is unimportant. At the same time, the behavior of the young intern should caution us. Truth without love can be willful, cruel and destructive.

The Church has no shortage of voices in these days demanding that the truth be heard. We could use a few more voices inviting the truth to be heard in love.

"For he is our peace, who has made us both one, and has broken down the dividing wall of hostility...reconciling us both to God in one body through the cross, thereby bringing the hostility to an end." Ephesians 2:14

The former Black Panther radical, Eldridge Cleaver, traveled the world from one communist country to another. During these travels, his eyes were opened. Racism, cruelty, oppression, and corruption were at least as prevalent, if not more so in these countries. He began to realize that calling racism a black-white issue was to miss the point. He began to grasp the comprehensive nature of the human dilemma. This was the painful but inescapable truth that Eldridge Cleaver came to see as he traveled the world: racism and injustice are equal opportunity employers.

The enforcement of quotas and legislation designed to combat injustice will never result in people openly and freely loving one another. These measures are damage control, at best. What people need is a power that can reconcile, actually bring them together- a power that can erase the past, free the present and open the future.

A painting came up for auction at an upscale art gallery. The technique was masterful, the colors vivid and alive. But it was the subject that left some viewers touched, others dismayed. The painting was of two men, one black, one white. They were kneeling, with two hands clasped and the other two touching the base of the Cross. Their eyes looked up at the crucified Jesus. The painting was entitled, 'Reconciled.'

Our reconciliation with one another must begin at the Cross because the One whom we have wronged, above anyone else, is God Himself. When those forces that separate us are met by God's power, a new, reconciled life emerges. The forgiveness that is in Jesus Christ is that power.

**"Look carefully, then, how you walk, not as unwise men but as wise, making the most of the time, for the days are evil."
Ephesians 5:15**

Scripture and our experience in time reveal to us that life is lived against the backdrop of a critical, temporal situation. Saint Paul brings this home in the verse from Ephesians. Life is not a neutral "tabula rasa" on which we simply write our experience for good or for ill. The Biblical witness makes it clear that we live in a creation in which evil militates against us. "The days are evil," Saint Paul says.

There are many ways of describing this evil, to be sure. From the fiery images of the Bible's apocalyptic writings (Daniel and Revelation) to the modern insights of evil as manifest in complex human behavior and institutions. But however we describe it, evil is a force which works, day by day, to pervert and destroy God's good creation. Paul wants the Church to keep this firmly in mind.

As people of faith, therefore, we enter the realm of the day with our eyes wide open. There is no room in the Christian faith for the naive optimism of "Pollyanna." We embrace with gratitude the gift of each day conscious of its untried opportunities, but we do so under the sign of the Cross. We remember that like our Master Jesus, our faithful walk in time takes place in a largely faithless world. Sometimes our lives exhibit in thought, word and deed just how close at hand and powerful evil can be. Saint Paul once underscored this fact when he lamented the frequency with which he did the very things, as a Christian, he had resolved not to do (Romans 7).

Will we make the most of the time allotted to us? Of course not. That is part of what it means to be caught in the reality we call sin. We inevitably squander the gift of time in one way or another. But Jesus has overcome evil through His death on the Cross. That is the decisive thing for us. Because of Christ's victory, we know that time itself has been gathered up in His grace! So, Christian, "make the most of the time", that wonderful gift. But make even more of the greatest gift of all: the boundless grace of God that forgives sinners and bears with us in love through time and eternity!

Baptism

It is the concreteness of Baptism, the actual fact of it, that faith is mean to trust. To be saved by faith alone does not mean we must turn to our inner resources and conjure up a God to believe in. Faith is not centered in itself. Faith is not something we mysteriously get from somewhere. Faith is called forth by the external Word of God's promise in Word and sacrament. Faith is called forth by the message of the Cross. Faith looks at the Cross and sees it for what it is: dead Jesus making me dead. Faith look at the resurrection and sees it for what it is: alive Jesus making me alive. I look at baptism and see it for what it is: the place, the very place, where God declares me dead and alive with Jesus and for His sake.

The old self in us objects to this in the same way it wants to spiritualize the Cross and make faith itself a matter of inner choice. In fact, many Christians are skeptical of Baptism:" What about my response? Am I not free to reject? You don't mean to say that grace is irresistible? Is baptism enough? Surely proclaiming the forgiveness of cross and baptism together are too much of a risk. What if people abuse baptism, take it for granted, use it as an excuse for not being serious Christians," and so forth.

A Christianity that pre-supposes a free will does not know what to do with an external word of grace – with word and sacrament. But who are we to look at dead Jesus and then begrudge God's grace? God did not turn back. Is He going to call off His mercy now because of the ungodly? Because you are ungodly?

Your Baptism worked forgiveness of sins in you and where there is forgiveness of sins there is life and salvation and a real future. And God does not give up or back out on His promises. God is God, after all. He didn't raise dead Jesus to life because He had second thoughts about how foolish it all seemed or because He changed His mind about saving you. It is God who said "It is finished" through His dying lips for you. It is God, who in the water and word of baptism gives that foolish, offensive, glorious, liberating word of the Cross – for you. So, dear Christian, remember your baptism daily. For it was in that God-ordained action that all the benefits of the Gospel were freely given to you.

"Therefore I say to you, the kingdom of God will be taken away from you and given to a people, producing the fruit of it."
Matthew 21:43

Western Europe and the United States are the principle inheritors of Christian civilization - or what is left of it. Christendom is largely a thing of the past. Gone are the days when villages and towns were dominated by the presence of Christian churches, and, more importantly, when the Christian story gave shape to all aspects of life. Today, Western, secular societies are a salad bar of religions, cultures and ideologies which pose a direct challenge to the Christian faith. For millions, one's worth is measured by one's capacity for acquisition and consumption of things. The pagan eroticism of the pop/entertainment culture has cheapened much of our common life. An aggressive scientism is attempting to strip life of any meaning beyond the rational, the technical and measurable.

Every generation is a time of challenge and decision for the Christian faith, and that means for local congregations and people who confess Jesus as Lord of all. Our time is no exception. The Christian faith is always one generation away from extinction. Ruined and empty church buildings are a reminder that we have no right to the kingdom. It is God's gift to us. So, we pray that His kingdom might prosper among us and that the fruit of that Kingdom may issue forth in a joyful, daring witness to the salvation that is in Jesus Christ.

"For we do not preach ourselves but Christ Jesus as Lord,." 2 Corinthians 4:5

The world is full of agendas. I have them, and so do you. There is a story told about a man who joined a congregation. He was eventually elected to the church council where he belligerently began to push his own ideas about what the church should be doing. After a year or so he called on the pastor and announced that he was leaving the congregation. Since he could not get his way, he was moving on.

Over the long centuries, many agendas have threatened to overwhelm the essential business of the Church. Occasionally they have succeeded, at least temporarily. At times, political agendas have dominated. This was especially true during the centuries following the collapse of the Roman empire. The church found itself holding the reigns of political power. The resulting abuses were predictable. At other times, the moral agenda has threatened to replace the Gospel with Law. Today, advocacy of the latest social agenda has become the de facto gospel in many churches.

Of course, none of this is new. Saint Paul found himself, again and again, having to remediate congregations and individuals under his care. His theme was constant: Christ and His cross must be central. Fifteen centuries later, Martin Luther took up the same Gospel cause.

The painter Lucas Cranach was a friend and supporter of Martin Luther and many of his works were in support of Reformation themes. Cranach painted the crucified Christ just above the altar table at City Church in Wittenberg, Germany, directly in front of where the preacher stands. He has depicted Martin Luther preaching, with one hand on the Bible and the other pointed toward Jesus Christ crucified at the center of the painting. Cranach is clarifying the agenda and making it clear to those called to preach, and to the congregation, that Jesus Christ crucified is the Church's agenda and the proper subject of the Church's preaching.

As long as the Church exists in time, God's people will be tempted to replace God's agenda with our own. But thanks be to God that He keeps hold of His Church in love and brings us back to Christ, whose agenda is to love sinners and bring them, at last, out of death to life.

"In Him all things hold together." Colossians 1:17

"Connect" is a popular word these days. Its use reflects a variety of contexts, but the goal is the same: to join together, to link, to bridge a gap, to cohere. The wide usage of the term is meant to speak into a world that is disconnected. People are looking for meaningful connections, because life is about connections. We need to be connected. But where do I look? Where do I find them? Marketing types have picked up on this. Thus, the appeal goes out: "Get Connected" through our product, service, etc.

"In Christ all things hold together," Paul wrote to the Colossian church. Another translation for "hold together" is "cohere". I like that. When Christ Jesus takes hold of life He brings real connection, real cohesion. The self comes to rest in its own skin. I see the whole creation as gift, with all the implications that awareness brings. Nor are the most tragic and apparently godless of circumstances outside the cohesive power of God's grace. Remember Paul's words to the Romans? "All things work together for good for those who love God and are called according to His purposes."

Many of life's connections are temporary, break under pressure or turn out to be forms of manipulation. Not so the connection with God in Christ. In Him, the broken fragments of our lives are brought together in the cohesion of love and mercy. To be held in the love of Christ is to be truly connected.

"Blessed be the God and Father of our Lord Jesus Christ, who according to His great mercy has caused us to be born again to a living hope through the resurrection of Jesus Christ from the dead, to obtain an inheritance which is imperishable and undefiled and will not fade away, reserved in heaven for you." 1 Peter 1:3

A TV commercial spoke of how using a particular product supports a "sustainable future." This phrase has become more common in recent years. Is the future "sustainable?" I suppose it depends on what future we are talking about.

If we are referring to the management of natural resources, in the short term, there is room for discussing sustainability. Good stewardship of the earth's resources is in everyone's best interest. To work for a "sustainable" environment is simply a matter of good stewardship. Nothing more and nothing less.

But some of the current rhetoric surrounding "sustainability" is also saying something else. Namely, that there is no future beyond what we can create for ourselves in this world. There is nothing beyond what we can see and experience. In this respect, the language of sustainability is competing for a view of the world and of existence which may be utterly devoid of God and authentic hope.

Christian hope is not rooted in human efforts at environmental management, in our capacities to bring about a "sustainable future". A closer look at even what science says about the future of the created universe is that it is ultimately unsustainable. Theories may vary. "Is the universe collapsing in on itself? Is it flying apart?" It hardly matters. The outcome is the same. Your life, the world, and the universe are not progressing, they are coming to an end.

It was to secure a real future that Christ Jesus died on the Cross and was raised for you. In Christ, God has promised to be there when the unsustainability of your life proves itself in death. Then He will raise you from the dead and usher His people into the joy of the new creation, "...to obtain an inheritance which is imperishable and undefiled and will not fade away, reserved in heaven for you".

There is a truly sustainable future. And God alone will bring it.

"May you be strengthened with all power, according to his glorious might, for all endurance and patience with joy." Colossians 1:11

The Sawyer Glaciers are located at the end of the Tracy Arm Fjord in Alaska. These massive rivers of ice and snow crawl along slowly, their movement virtually imperceptible. Slow as they may be, however, they are irresistible. Everything before them is swept away, and the effects of their progress are permanent, their purpose inevitably fulfilled.

Most of us grow impatient if we have to wait too long. You have probably been in line for groceries and seen how much abuse the check stand servers have to endure at the hands of impatient shoppers, through no fault of their own. Having to wait can bring out the worst in us. Waiting can be hard, long, tiring and aggravating.

For the Christian, waiting is the matrix in which faith grows. Waiting keeps us grounded in the here and now and focused on the opportunities for living that each day brings us. In waiting, we learn that walking, not running, is the proper pace of living. At times, when our needs and longings seem too much for us, we can grow impatient with what appears to be God's slowness to act. At those times it may be helpful to remember that creation rides on God's glacial purposes. The power and inevitability with which they move are staggering, beyond us.

Therefore, on this new day of grace, take up Paul's prayer as your own. Pray that God's power and might may translate into your life as endurance and patience, keeping you in the faith and confident that His purposes in Christ Jesus are carrying you along, just as surely as those rivers of ice, imperceptibly yet inevitably, flow into the sea.

"Thanks be to God for His inexpressible gift!" 2 Corinthians 9:15

A friend was helping clean out the house of an elderly man as he prepared for a move into more manageable accommodations. He picked up a small piece of wood that had fallen onto the floor and tossed it into a nearby waste basket. "Oh, no!", said the elderly man, "Don't throw that away." His friend was puzzled. It was just a scrap of wood. Then he heard the story.

The old man recalled a day, years ago. He and the woman who would become his wife for over 70 years, had spent an afternoon strolling along a lake shore. It was the first day they had met. They spoke of their lives, inquiring after one another, getting to know one another. The shoreline was strewn with small bits of driftwood which they would casually pick up and toss out onto the water. Within a few months they were married. One year later, on their first anniversary, she gave him a small box tied with a ribbon. Inside was a piece of driftwood she had kept as a reminder of that first day. It was her gift to him.

The friend reached into the waste basket, retrieved the piece of wood and reverently handed it to the elderly man. Something had changed. The friend now saw more than a scrap of wood. He saw the gift.

You and I were born into a world where everything has been provided, including life itself. Sin reveals itself in us when we see life's gifts only as things to be selfishly used, manipulated, then cast aside. Many treat life this way, sometimes out of ignorance, sometimes willfully. Then they hear the story, the story of God in Jesus Christ. They hear of His love, His mercy, His deep concern for their lostness. They hear the story of His Cross and Resurrection. And when the Holy Spirit brings this old, old story of Jesus and His love to life in us, something changes. We begin to see the gift in everything because we have seen the greatest gift of all-Jesus Christ our Lord.

"Timothy my fellow worker greets you, and so do Lucius and Jason and Sosipater, my kinsmen." Romans 16:21

The greeting above comes at the end of Paul's letter to the Romans. We do not know much about the people he mentions, but we do know they were with him. And this is significant. In nearly all of his letters, Paul references someone who accompanies him on his journeys, supporting him in his work. He gives thanks, by name, for individuals in congregations. He expresses gratitude for their support, for their efforts on behalf of the Gospel.

When I think back on the people I have served, I don't remember them all. But I do remember many of those, by name, who actively served with me in ministry.

The life of any congregation is made up of the participation, commitment and involvement of persons. The first few generations of Christian people did not have church buildings, constitutions and bylaws, business plans, or programs. They had each other. And their communities were not centered around their perceived needs, comfortable worship schedules or a salad bar of programs and activities. They were centered around the new life in the Spirit that had taken hold of them in Jesus Christ as they heard the message of the Cross and Resurrection. Against pressures from their families, society at large, and often at great personal risk, they gathered together in joy and gratitude for worship, witness, learning, and service.

The institutional character of today's Church can obscure something important. At its heart the church is a community of persons in relationship: in relationship to Christ through Word and sacrament, in relationship to one another through faith, hope, and love, the gifts of the Holy Spirit. Paul's mentioning of people by name was certainly not meant to slight others. But in mentioning them, he reminds us of our relatedness in Christ and how important it is to love and support one another.

No Apologies

In Matthew 28, our Lord Jesus issued his final command and promise to his disciples. These words represent the "marching orders" of the Church. Sometimes they are called the "Great Commission". Significantly, Baptism has a prominent place in our Lord's command.

The first thing to note about our Lord's words is that they are a command. Baptism, therefore, is not an option the Church or the Christian can take or leave. We are not to despise Baptism or treat it lightly. Neither are we to speculate on what happens to those who are not baptized. As followers of Jesus, our job is to carry out His command. He will deal with the exceptions. After all, Jesus stated, "I am the way, the truth, and the life. No one comes to the Father but by me." Although this text is often quoted as a condition that people must meet to be saved, that is not what the text actually says. The text says that Christ will decide who has access to the Father. How Christ will handle those who do not receive Baptism is His business. Our business is to baptize, as He has commanded.

The most important words in Jesus command are these: "In the name of the Father and of the Son and of the Holy Spirit." We baptize with water together with God's name. It is not our word (our decision to repent and follow Christ) that is added to the water (as in what some call "believer's baptism"). In Baptism, God adds His word to the water. That is why the Lord includes the Triune name of God along with His command to baptize. He wants the Christian to know and trust that in Baptism, God promises to give you His name. This is the central promise God gives you in Baptism. This is the promise that we are called to trust, in which we place faith. It is a promise designed to comfort and encourage sinners.

Though some may challenge it, you don't have to apologize for your Baptism. God has promised in Baptism to be your God, to identify you with everything He has done for your salvation in Jesus Christ, to give you the forgiveness of sins, life and salvation. In Baptism, God has made a decision for you.

"By this we shall know that we are of the truth, and reassure our hearts before Him whenever our hearts condemn us; for God is greater than our hearts." 1 John 3:20

The letter of 1 John reminds us that love shows itself in action. But what if it does not? What about those times when we look inside ourselves and have to face the truth that we have not lived up to the great commandment?

I knew a Christian woman years ago who was obsessed with how unloving she was. She complained about it, lamented it, wore it like a thorny crown. Her own sinful heart became her prosecutor. I said to her, "The way you carry on, you would think that your sinful heart is greater than Jesus your Savior."

God is greater than our hearts. Our hearts may prosecute us, but God is our judge, He sees through us and knows us. God knows our spiritual condition, and He knows that the measure of love we do have in our hearts, born of faith, means that we have passed from death to life. Although we are imperfect in love - and our hearts will tell us this - we are, nevertheless, born of God's great love in Jesus and we are His beloved children. Now, there is something to be obsessed about!

"And this is not your own doing; it is the gift of God." Ephesians 2:8

Our time has been called the "Information Age". For many, the key to the human future is knowledge. Knowledge will power us to a utopian future, they say.

For others, power itself is what matters. Power in the form of money, political leverage, military might, the capacity to wheel and deal and acquire wealth. Life coaching types make millions off the promise of helping people discover and apply "personal power", which is supposed to unleash one's power to achieve success, however defined. The world is obsessed with knowledge and power as the levers that will bring us the life we want. We see it all around us and in ourselves.

You were created in the image of God. The Bible tells us so and this is a high calling. Therefore, the fact that knowledge and power preoccupy us is no accident. They are supreme gifts that distinguish us among all creatures. God is all-powerful, and He has given you some power. God is all knowing, and has given you some knowledge.

But there is are other characteristics of God for which you were also made and they are more important by far than the other two: holiness and righteousness. God is all-holy, we are not holy. God is all-righteous, we are not. This, not the lack of knowledge or power, is the great human tragedy. When the awesome gifts of knowledge and power are in the hands of a creature that lacks these most important qualities God has given us, His very holiness, those gifts become tainted, and our lives and the world look the way they do. And we have no solution.

In a miracle of love and mercy, God has determined that His holiness and righteousness are His gift to us through faith in Christ. It is this faith, not what we know or are able to do, that restores us to our Creator, the world and ourselves. Why has God done this? Is some remnant of righteousness left in us that makes us worth loving? Hardly. God loves us not because of who we are but in spite of us. His love is sheer, undeserved gift. The Bible's word for it is grace. Our knowledge and power will not save us. The grace of God in Christ Jesus will.

"God is love." 1 John 4:8

A family moved in across the street from a friend of mine. The new neighbor waved smilingly each time he saw my friends. That is, until one day when this new fellow approached my friend and asked him if he needed any help with life insurance. My friend said no, he was well taken care of in that area. The new neighbor smiled and went home. After that day the waving stopped.

It is important for me to know that even if God gets very little done with me, He loves me nonetheless. In fact, it is truly a travesty when we use love.

Our language does not have a word for God's love. The ancient Greek language of the New Testament does. That word is, 'agape', which may be translated, 'undeserved' or 'unmerited love'.

The love of God is an end in itself. He does not use it for other purposes. He does not love us in order to save us or change us or do something to us. If God accomplishes nothing with us He loves us still. God loves His children that are forever lost to Him as much as He loves those who have come home. God does not use His love to get something done. This is part of what it means to say, "God is love". God's love is not an emotion or a feeling. It is not a responsive love that is attracted to the beautiful and repelled by the ugly. It does not calculate or count the cost.

A Coast Guard captain called for his crew to launch their ship into a terrible storm. A ship was foundering, and the distress signal had gone out. One of the crewmen objected. "Captain", he said,"If we sail out into that gale we may never come back." The captain replied, "Getting back is not our chief concern. Getting to that ship is."

The love of God in the Church, reflected in His people, is not an instrument. It is an end in itself. We are not to seek the welfare of others so that they will join our church or give money to the church or think well of the church. God loves and that is it. And His people are called to love, whether it achieves anything or not.

"For Us and for our Salvation he came down from heaven"

Some contemporary versions of the Christian faith would suggest that God has come among us to serve as the ultimate life coach, and that the Bible is little more than a manual for creating a successful life. God's job is to boost us into the saddle of life and we complete the job by putting in a little free-will effort of our own. It is not hard to understand this emphasis. We are masters at making everything about us. At the same time the Christian message *is* about us... but in a very different sense.

"For Us and for our Salvation he came down from heaven." So we believe and confess in the words of the ancient Creed. It was for us that He came. Specifically, for our salvation. This is the mighty work of God to which the Bible, in all it's parts, bears witness. God has acted to save a lost world, and that includes lost me and lost you, confounded in our pretensions, tangled up in our wants and ultimately powerless against the powers that are set against us. Under such circumstances we don't need life coaching to send us back to ourselves, we need salvation from outside ourselves. And so, it was "For us and our salvation" that God in Jesus the Savior came.

And He continues to come, generation after generation. He comes in the Word of His glorious Gospel by which Word sinners are forgiven. He comes in the Sacraments – Baptism and Holy Communion – whereby He takes us in His loving embrace, the firm grip of His grace, and promises to never leave us or forsake us. He comes in the midst of life, powerfully and mysteriously guiding the affairs of nations and every life – and that means your life - according to His good and gracious will. Not because you have willed it but because He has willed it for you in Christ Jesus!

"...as we await our blessed hope, the appearing of our great God and Savior Jesus Christ..." Titus 2:13

Whatever happened to whistling? You just do not hear it anymore. I cannot account for it completely, but I have some idea as to what has happened, and why it matters.

When my great-grandfather was serving his congregation in southwestern Minnesota at the opening of the twentieth century, events in Moscow, Bangkok or anywhere else in the far-flung world did not preoccupy him, if he knew of them at all. The aches and pains of the world which did occupy him were mostly local, very close to home. There was a kind of immediacy to life. The scale of life was manageable.

Now, over a century later, the aches and pains of the entire world are broadcast into our lives instantaneously. Media cultures around the world are rubbing our noses in every imaginable dysfunction, tragedy and outrage. Predictably, the humor of such an age is accompanied by the handmaidens of hopelessness - vulgarity and cynicism. Whistling requires a light touch, an easy-going sense of humor. Why should anyone be whistling in the face of such a chaotic and crazy world? So, my argument is that whistling has become a casualty of the self-polluting of the contemporary human environment. It is a small symptom of a larger illness.

Can we have an authentic sense of humor, devoid of cynicism, in such a world? I think so. It is in the gap between what we are and what we ought to be where both tragedy and comedy dwell. Christians are very much aware of this gap. We know that gap to be the result of sin, our separation from God, one another and the creation. Apart from the framework of that "blessed hope" that is in Christ Jesus, it is hard to face this gap without trending toward cynicism, even despair.

In Christ, God has closed the gap between Himself and our sin. What this means for you as a Christian is that you can face the disparities in your life and the world in the light of God's grace. And as you reflect on that grace, and all the promise and blessed hope it holds because of Christ Jesus, it may even get you to whistling once in a while!

"...that you may know what is the hope to which he has called you, what are the riches of his glorious inheritance in the saints, and what is the immeasurable greatness of his power in us who believe, according to the working of his great might which he accomplished in Christ when he raised him from the dead and made him sit at his right hand in the heavenly places, far above all rule and authority and power and dominion, and above every name that is named, not only in this age but also in that which is to come..." Ephesians 1:18-19

While on vacation, a man went canoeing on a river that was unknown to him. He paddled for a long time, enjoying the landscape until he began to feel the current accelerating. As the canoe picked up speed, it suddenly hit a submerged rock, jarring the paddle loose from the man's hands. He watched helplessly as it floated away. Then, his ear caught the sound of roaring water up ahead. The canoe was heading toward a waterfall.

One of the contradictions of our time is, on the one hand, the progress of technology and science and, on the other, the sense that humanity has reached a point where the problems, the chaotic difficulties we face, may be too much for us. The world has gotten out of control, and we may not be able to pull it back. There have been voices in recent decades suggesting that, like the dinosaurs, humanity's time on this planet may be coming to an end.

We do face an uncertain future. But when has it not been so? No generation has been given a road map for tomorrow. Each day must be received in trust, in faith. Faith trusts that no matter how ominous the future may appear to be, it will always resolve into the purposes of God.

The gospels tell the story of the ascension of Jesus into heaven where He is seated at the right hand of the Father. From this place of power and authority, the Bible tells us, Christ holds the reigns of history, and your life, in His hands. You may not have the assurance of knowing where you are going, but you can be assured that the currents beneath you flow out of His good and gracious purposes.

"Do not be conformed to this world, but be transformed..."
Romans 12:2

If I want to take the measure of the temperature in our house, I look at the thermometer. If the temperature is not to my liking, I am not obligated to live with it. I have the option of adjusting the thermostat.

Jesus had some specific words for those in whom faith is a living reality. He called them "salt" and "light." When these things are present, the temperature of life is adjusted to the atmospherics of the kingdom. Or, to use Paul's words, the Christian is not a conformer but a transformer.

At the same time, it is important to point out that the New Testament authors do not put out a call for deliberate social transformation. The New Testament is no Communist Manifesto. Saint Paul and the others were not offering a program designed to turn Christians into a legion of social workers. As often as not the Christian life transforms because it's intent is not to transform. Why? Because Christians are called to continually adjust life to the atmospherics of the kingdom. If I am in business and am tempted or even ordered to perform in a dishonest fashion, my Christian duty is not to conform to the dishonesty. I am under no obligation to get along with anyone who invites me to conform in this way.

Simply reflecting the status quo in life is not the way of the Christian. Our lives are tempered not by the latest expedient but by the Word of God as we hear the Law and the Gospel and receive the sacraments, as Christ Jesus conforms us to Himself. The culture offers this formula: "Go along in order to get along." Our faith reminds us, "You are not a thermometer. You are a thermostat."

"It is God who justifies; who is to condemn? Is it Christ Jesus, who died, yes, who was raised from the dead, who is at the right hand of God, who indeed intercedes for us?" Romans 8:33

Two young people were walking along in front of me in a local retail store. They were speaking quietly when suddenly, one of them turned to the other and in a loud voice exclaimed, "Don't you judge me!"

No one likes to be judged, of course. In fact, we can construct vast systems of rationalization to justify our own thoughts, words and actions which tend to deflect, in our minds, the need to be judged. You might need judging, but not me! But if our lives are not worth judging, they cannot be worth much.

Animals don't build courtrooms and hold trials. Creatures who live according to unerring instincts and to which they are bound cannot be held accountable. The same cannot be said for you. You were created in the image of God. This means you have attributes which enable you to share in the management, the stewardship of creation. Although limited, God has given you power and knowledge which are of such importance that you are held accountable for how you use them. Among the parables of Jesus in the New Testament, parables addressing stewardship are the most common. And the motif of judgment is in them all.

Linda and I spent part of a day at the Orange County Fair. We strolled among the exhibits and enjoyed the people watching. At one point, we stopped for a break at one of the many refreshment stands, chatting with the woman who prepared our food. She asked me what I did for a living. I indicated that I was a pastor. She immediately commented, in a rather worried tone, about what the last judgment might be like. Obviously, it was on her mind. I looked her in the eye and said, "Remember this. The One who will judge you is the One who died for you." Her mouth fell open. "I've never heard that before," she said with a smile.

Left to ourselves there is little upon which to base a gentle judgment at the end of life. There is simply too much evidence against us. But Jesus, your Savior, friend and brother, will be on the bench, and He has already spoken: "Father, forgive them..."

"For freedom Christ has set us free." Galatians 5:1

If you have read the novel or seen the movie Ben Hur, you will remember the insight it gave into the life of a galley slave, chained to his oar, year after year. If the ship should sink, he would drown like a rat with no way of escape. Freedom is what the slave longed for. Death in bondage is what usually came.

In the case of Ben Hur, the events that freed him from a pitiless life did not result in true freedom, not right away. He went on to be adopted by the Roman admiral whose life he saved. Power and wealth now accompanied his freedom from the galleys. But he was not free. His life was consumed by hatred of the man who had unjustly condemned him. He remained bound to sin.

Freedom is not being able to do what you want, having independent wealth or simply following your appetites and desires. To be truly free is to be set free from our bondage to sin. Ben Hur did not know what freedom was until the grace of God in Christ took hold of him and he was able to forgive. Author Lew Wallace was making this seminal point in his great novel.

Ben Hur goes on to become a member of the Christian community and eventually assists in bringing support to the persecuted Christians in Rome. He and some fellow-Christians form an underground church in the catacombs outside the city where they gather to celebrate, in the midst of death, the life and freedom that was theirs in Christ.

This is how the Christian, born a slave to sin, regards the Gospel of Christ. In Jesus Christ we find and celebrate our true freedom from sin's captivity unto death and our new life as children of God even unto eternal life.

"I was once alive apart from the law, but when the commandment came, sin revived, and I died;" Romans 7:9

Once there was a young man named John who enjoyed the piano. And while he had never received formal training, he considered himself to be on the level of a concert pianist. In fact, he could not read music and what he did play by ear was at the most elementary level. For a time his friends indulged him. But as time went on his illusions began to dominate his life. John spent hour upon hour playing, never advancing in his ability. He was losing himself in his illusions. He began to speak of his plans to give concerts, to go on tour. In preparation, John went deeply into debt and purchased an expensive concert grand piano, and invited his friends over for a 'concert' on the new instrument.

The appointed evening came, the friends gathered and John stumbled through several songs. The quality of the instrument could not compensate for the embarrassment of his poor playing. Then, his best friend introduced a young woman who had accompanied him. Would John mind if his guest played something? Reluctantly, the host slipped off the piano bench. The woman took her place and for the next few minutes, the piano came alive with the extraordinary sound of Mozart. Her playing was at the highest level. In fact, she was an accomplished pianist. John was shattered. When John heard the woman play, it was not beautiful, it was the sound of death to him.

God loves us too much to leave us to ourselves. He uses His law to bring us to spiritual sobriety. But his goal is not to leave us there. In the months that followed, the young woman voluntarily became John's tutor. John slowly and with difficulty emerged from his illusions. He came under the structure of her discipline. More importantly, he came to see how much she cared for him. He came under the influence of her love. In time, they married.

The path to seeing the greatness of Christ begins at the place of your great need. God's law exposes that need. To shatter you? Yes. But more importantly, to bring you to see the extraordinary greatness of God's love for you in Christ Jesus.

"Now may the Lord of peace himself give you peace at all times and in every way." 2Thessalonians 3:16

While visiting Florence, Italy, several years ago I spoke with a woman who had made her first visit there. I asked her if she planned on returning. "Why?", she replied, I have been here for a week and have seen everything." On that same trip to Florence, I met a man in the Uffizi gallery, which contains one of the world's great art collections. He was visiting from England and had been sitting in front of paintings in one room of the gallery, eight hours a day, for a week.

The human scramble to outrun boredom has reached a new level of intensity in our time. In Southern California where we live, frantic activity is part of the character of life. There is actually very little community here. The perpetual motion of this place creates the illusion of community, that is all. As people pile experience upon experience, however, it becomes apparent that this does not decrease boredom but only intensifies it. Our shallow revulsion of the routine masks a deeper anxiety. The new and the novel, devoid of vision, passion, and meaning reveal an emptiness that all the experiences in the world cannot address. What are we looking for anyway?

Three stonemasons were hard at work. Each was asked what he was doing. The first grumbled, "I am cutting stone." The second answered with indifference, "I am making money." The third man smiled with a bright eye and said, "I am building a cathedral!" For him, the routine of laying stone had a kind of glory attached to it. With each stone, he saw the larger vision emerging.

When the love of God in Christ opens the heart, our restless anxiety is brought to rest. The routine and the ordinary are invested with eternal meaning. The scope of life shifts. The little things matter. Knowing we are loved and forgiven gives us back to ourselves and to others with new eyes. The routines of life become the little liturgies by whose repetitions life unfolds as the ever-new and renewing gift of God's grace.

"Rejoice in the Lord always. Again, I say, rejoice!" Philippians 4:4

There can be so much wrong with the world and our lives, it hardly seems right to speak of joy. It is a bit like a family preparing to gather for a wedding only to receive the news that the bride has come down with cancer. A pall is cast over everyone. How can there be room for joy in this?

When the Bible gives us the picture of Adam and Eve, before disobedience ravaged them, three things are apparent. First, and most importantly, they were absorbed in the goodness and greatness of God. Secondly, they found delight in the garden, in the creation. Thirdly, they were lost in one another. What is important to see here is that Adam and Eve lacked self-consciousness. They were conscious of what was outside the self. When sin entered in, all they could see was themselves. They hid their nakedness and literally attempted to hide from God. And among the great casualties in all of this was joy.

Jesus Christ came to restore us to God, to the creation and to one another. This means that if joy is to be found in this life, it will be found on these three fronts and not in an intensification of self-discovery. This is precisely why there is so little joy in the world today. The more the self examines itself, the more elusive joy becomes.

Saint Paul, sitting in a Roman jail cell, could encourage Christians to "Rejoice in the Lord always. Again, I say, rejoice." In the Lord Jesus Paul had been restored to God, the deepest source of joy. The difficulties in the temporal circumstances of his life could not overwhelm this joy.

Focusing on the self, at the expense of everything else in life, is a formula for chronic unease and joylessness. Multiply these selves into the millions and you have some idea as to why human life in general, and perhaps your life, looks the way it does. Without Christ, life is a joyless, hopeless quest to resolve myself within myself. With Christ, life rings with an authentic joy now - rooted in Him - that will be brought to perfection in the life to come.

"Love does no wrong to a neighbor, therefore love is the fulfilling of the law." Romans 13:10

To love is to fulfill the law. There is no law against love. There are degrees and kinds of love, to be sure. But not to love? That is not an option. The question is, do we love well or badly? This, in fact, is our problem. From birth the human will is engaged in loving. It has no option, no choice in the matter. What becomes readily apparent is that self-love is the focus. So, in a very real sense, we have no so-called 'free will' to love or not love - God or anyone else. The myriad dysfunctions of the world are all the evidence we need to conclude that bad love is the way with human beings. Oh, there will be variations toward the good, and many are quite adept at keeping their bad love to themselves, but from birth, the die is cast; human beings are bad lovers. They are bound to be.

This predisposition to bad love is what the bible calls 'sin', the turning in on the self. Asking the bound will to free itself from this mess does nothing. If you are bound, you must be set free, from outside yourself. So enters the Gospel.

Saint Paul wrote that you and I might find it in ourselves to crank up sacrificial love for someone we consider worthy - maybe. But God shows His love for us in that "...while we were yet sinners, Christ died for us." The love of God is perfect. God really and truly loves. And this is made supremely clear in Jesus our Lord, who gave Himself for the unlovely, for the bad lovers.

This is the Good News! God's will to love the bad lover is what we call grace. In mercy and love, for Christ's sake, God simply declares the bound sinner, the bad lover, free as an act of sheer mercy and grace. Someone once called it "amazing". And so it is.

"Suppose one of you has a hundred sheep and loses one of them. "Doesn't he leave the ninety-nine in the open country and go after the lost sheep until he finds it?" Luke 15:4

She turned the house upside down. After days of searching, in between the usual routines of living, she finally found it, clutching it against her breast in tears. No, it wasn't a nine-carat diamond ring or a winning lottery ticket. It was an old fountain pen, tarnished by time and no longer serviceable. During their college years, her husband wrote her every day they were apart with this pen. The letters, carefully wrapped in a bundle, had been destroyed in a fire years before, not long after her husband's death. The pen was all she had to remind her of those letters.

On the surface, of course, there was no value to be perceived in this old writing instrument. To anyone else the old pen was fit for nothing but to be discarded. But for her it represented the one she had loved and who loved her.

The story of the Good Shepherd goes even further. Unlike the pen in the story above, there is nothing intrinsically lovable in us that God should seek us. This can come as something of a shock to a creature that is convinced it is the center of the universe. The fact is that human beings are expendable assets in this world and not all that lovable. The self-righteous who heard Jesus tell this story had long since convinced themselves that they were better off without those who wandered away from righteousness. Good riddance. They also might have questioned the wisdom of leaving ninety-nine sheep defenseless, to search for one. Is not a bird in the hand worth two in the bush? The math does not work! Well, maybe not in our calculations but God's math is different. It is the mathematics of grace.

The Good Lord does not wait for us to make our way back to Him. Not only can we not do so, we do not want to do so. The Good News is that God seeks us in our bondage to sin, in our lostness. God has taken the initiative not because He has lost something that in and of itself has infinite worth, but because He chooses to do so, out of sheer grace and mercy. Thanks be to God!

"Let us look to Jesus the pioneer and perfecter of our faith, who for the joy that was set before him endured the cross, despising the shame, and is seated at the right hand of the throne of God." Hebrews 12:2

Just around the corner from the famous Pantheon in Rome is the church of Santa Maria Sopra Minerva, built on the site of an ancient temple to the goddess Minerva, thus the name (Saint Mary on Minerva). The church is distinctive in several ways: it is the only Gothic style church in Rome, and it contains the burial place of Saint Catherine of Siena (minus her head which sits in Siena). The church also contains works by Fra Angelico, Bernini, and the statue by Michaelangelo, Christ the Redeemer.

Michaelangelo's design captures something of what the writer to the Hebrews proclaims. The great sculptor depicts the risen Christ embracing the Cross and the other instruments of His passion. Yet even here, after the Resurrection, the Lord's face is turned away from the Cross, "despising its shame." Suffering and death are now subject to Him. The victory has been won and the promise of the new age to come is secure. Now Christ Jesus is seated at the right hand of the Father, the place of power- language which underscores the certainty that God's work of Redemption will be carried to completion.

It is fitting, it seems to me, that this depiction of the Risen Christ should embrace the cross. For the message of the Gospel - Christ crucified and risen for sinners-is now the instrument used by the Risen Lord to call, gather, enlighten and sanctify the faithful. Jesus has turned the tables. Now suffering and death, though no less real, have lost their hold, their sting. Although in this old age of sin we must endure suffering and death, the crucified and Risen Lord assures us that the new age has begun. One day, on that great and glorious Day, the work of Redemption will be complete and "the pioneer and perfecter of our faith" will lead us into the joys of God's eternal kingdom.

The Temple

In my church study is a tattered songbook. Here is the story. The year was 1983. The place was a youth hostel in Leipzig, East Germany. As we sat talking at our tables after dinner our tour group leader, Pastor Herb Brokering, came over and whispered quietly in my ear to follow him. As we walked down a long hallway, Herb motioned to keep silent then quickly opened the door to what turned out to be a very large linen closet. There, sitting on a small stool, was a smiling young girl who had greeted us earlier in the evening. We sat down and Herb, who spoke fluent German, introduced us. Her name was Gerlinde. On her lap were a guitar and a small, worn songbook.

Gerlinde began to speak as Herb translated. When she heard a group of Christians would be staying at the hostel, she was overjoyed. She was a Christian and was praying for an opportunity to share something of her faith with us. But there was a need to be careful. The others who worked there were not Christian. Some were quite hostile to the faith and would be quick to report her. But she was willing to take the risk. Here is the text to the first song Gerlinde sang for us that evening.

The Temple
We are being built into a temple, a dwelling for our Holy God.
This house of the Lord is the congregation, the pillar, and the truth's foundation.
Shaped like beautiful gemstones, by His mercy through the Word, when we love and trust each other, the temple will grow more and more, then the temple will grow more and more.

Finally, sensing we had stayed about as long as we dare, the three of us prayed together and got up to leave. Gerlinde, her eyes filled with tears, pressed the little songbook into my hand. One by one we quietly slipped back into the hallway.

The next morning, our group gathered in the lobby after breakfast to await our bus. Herb and I were talking together when Gerlinde walked through the lobby carrying some towels. The three of us made eye contact and smiled. The Temple had grown a little more.

Good For Nothing

No one wants to hear the old slur, "You're a good for nothing!" Even those who live by exploitation, robbery or handouts take offense at such a comment. But the fact remains that to live in the world means you have to be good for something. God has set it up that way. To not contribute, to not carry your weight, is to call your worth and value into question. So, we learn from an early age. And because the world operates this way it is easy to assume that the same equation applies to our relationship with the Living God, and, in fact, it does. How human beings live, our thoughts, words and deeds, our works and ways matter.

We were made to love God and our neighbors as ourselves. That is our purpose, that is what we are good for (or should be), that is what justifies us, to use Paul's language. So, how are you doing? Want to boast about how well you are fulfilling the law of love? Neither do I. And if that is the case, the questions can rightly be asked of us, "What are you good for? If not for love, then what?"

Saint Paul knew the Abraham story well enough to realize that it was not Abraham's performance that made him a part of God's people and plans. God made promises to Abraham, and Abraham trusted those promises. End of story. Paul drew the proper theological conclusions from this and in the light of the Cross and Resurrection declared that faith is God's singular way with us, the ungodly, the good-for-nothings. Love does not save us. Faith saves us. And this is so for no other reason than that God would have it so! God gives us the righteousness of His beloved Son as a gift, by grace through faith, apart from our demonstrating that we have earned it or deserve it, and shows the world once and for all that He intends to run the world - and the future He will bring - according to His grace.

The light shines in the darkness, and the darkness has not overcome it." John 1:5

My late father, Rev. Carroll N. Anderson, wrote this devotional piece in 1959 for a Lutheran church publication while he was an Air Force chaplain, stationed in Hawaii.

Tonight as I am writing this, the midnight sky became as noon and the red rays of dawn seemed to appear in the West. What we in Honolulu have seen is the explosion of an atomic weapon over 700 miles away. That light filled each spectator with a cold sense of awe and wonder. This was the light of death.

Jesus is the true light who enlightens every person. Today, because men have refused His light, the night sky over the Pacific is turned to day – but only for a moment. The darkness that belongs in the night returns quickly.

The light and power of atomic weapons are beyond description. The power and light of Christ are much greater. A great city can be destroyed by a single bomb. Not one city can be built by a bomb. The light of Christ has the power to create new life in the repentant heart. The light of Christ shows you your sin and reveals to you your Savior.

No midnight darkness can overcome the radiance of the Christian life. No bomb can destroy the Christian's life in Christ.

This Sunday your congregation will be a special source of light in your community, as your pastor presents the light of Christ. Take that light with you all week.

Beware the Downward Pull

T. F. Gullixson was president of Luther Seminary, Saint Paul, Minnesota, during the middle years of the 20th century when my father was a student there. My father once recalled a sermon he heard T.F. Gullison preach entitled, "Beware the Downward Pull." The title speaks volumes.

In this impersonal age of technology, the conduct of the individual becomes less and less of an issue. All kinds of morally and ethically destructive behavior is tolerated, if not sanctioned. Someone has described life in these times with a heady phrase - 'chaotic syncretism'. That's a very erudite way of saying, "Anything goes." T. F. Gullixson was onto something. The gravitational effect of sin on human moral and ethical conduct is apparent. Someone once said, "Character is measured by what you do when no one is watching." How many of us could stand the scrutiny of our deeds done in the dark?

The new life in Christ is meant to redeem us from eternal death and free us for love of God and the neighbor. As Lutherans, we know that the Christian life is not a call to moral and ethical ladder climbing in order to make ourselves acceptable to God. We are, in the end, saved by grace through faith. At the same time, we are called to struggle with sin, to "beware the downward pull" of sin. For what is at stake is freedom, the costly freedom Christ has won for us on the Cross. When we allow our basest impulses, lusts, and desires to drag us down, we cheapen the life of freedom for love that God has given us. Such a self-centered life is of little good to itself or the neighbor. The writer of 1 John wanted more for those whom he cared about, "I am writing these things to you so that you might not sin." This little letter toward the end of the New Testament could easily be titled, "Beware the Downward Pull." Read it for yourself.

John also proclaims our Advocate to us, "Jesus Christ the Righteous." In our struggle to live out the freedom God has given us, we do and will give ample evidence of our sinfulness. But Christ Jesus has laid claim on sinners. He is our righteousness and will be so all the way to life's end. For the "downward pull" is not greater than the "upward call in Jesus Christ our Lord!"

"If we say that we have no sin, we deceive ourselves, and the truth is not in us." 1 John 1:8

Who am I? This most basic of questions demands a response, and every human being makes one. We answer this question largely by determining our own identity: I am who I choose to be. Yet our insistence on taking life into our own hands is easily distorted and becomes defining of what the Scriptures call 'sin' – that willful insistence on stealing my existence from God, and resolving every issue down to what I want.

The culture says that we are bundles of largely unrealized wonderfulness only inhibited by the myriad injustices foisted on us by others (who are, apparently, not so wonderful).

The Bible reveals God's assessment of the human to us. The defining word regarding what it means to be human does not rightly derive from us but the One who created us. And God says we are willful sinners, deserving of His wrath, in need of forgiveness. Small wonder humans flee from this God of wrath for all they are worth, preferring to "re-imagine" God in kinder, gentler forms.

If, however, there is no need to speak of the wrath of God, then there is not much need to talk about the sin that incurs the wrath. But this avoidance is no answer to the real problem of sin and all its consequences.

Christianity is incoherent without the idea of sin. There can be no good news of the Gospel without first understanding the bad news of sin. The mission of Jesus makes no sense if we remove such concepts from our thinking. Take away the doctrine of sin and we take away the doctrine of the Incarnation. Indeed, we take away the entire message of the New Testament.

Because we are born in the darkness of sin, we assume our blindness to be life in the light. But Christ Jesus died for sinners that we might walk in the "true light," Christ Himself. When we persist in our self-defining intransigence, we remain in our sins. When Christ opens our eyes through the Gospel by His amazing grace, we see our need for a savior and the Savior we need.

Waiting

Several years ago our family took a cruise in the Mediterranean. One of the stops along the way was the gritty, southern Italian port of Naples. After an early breakfast Linda and Kristin headed off to the beauties of the Amalfi coast while Erik, Geoff and I taxied off to exercise our historical imaginations at Pompeii and Herculaneum, the two cities devastated and preserved by the eruption of Mt. Vesuvius in 79 AD.

Walking those ancient streets is something one does not soon forget. Pompeii is impressive in the sheer scale of its ruins. Herculaneum, just a few miles away, has an intimacy and immediacy that has one asking, "Where did everybody go?"

As we wandered through the streets, homes and public buildings a kind of sadness became palpable. The remnants of ancient lives were all around us. But now the business of living is silent in these places. Instead of living communities, these places are fields of ruins which the current living community is struggling to preserve against the inevitable ravages of time.

These ancient places stand in mute testimony to the reality of the human future. In the last analysis, the world and our lives are not progressing, they are coming to an end. This is the judgment of the Cross upon us all. There is no abiding city here. Perhaps God has arranged things in such a way that Pompeii, Herculaneum, and their counterparts world-wide, are meant to remind us of just this.

The writer to the Hebrews had seen this centuries ago. "There is no lasting city here...," he wrote. So, we wait. We wait when it is long and tiring to wait. We wait when it is hard to wait. In the closing days of His earthly life, our Lord Jesus said it Himself, "Heaven and earth will pass away, but my word will never pass away." We wait because God will keep His promise.

"In the world you will have trouble." John 16:33

To be in the hands of the Living God is no guarantee of exemption from the stresses and perils of life. Far from it. Our Lord Jesus gave the rather sobering news to His disciples that "in the world, you will have trouble.." As long as we are in this life, troubles will come, in all shapes and sizes. Knowing this is one thing, but having to face them, endure them, suffer them, is another. It can be just too much. Our Lord Jesus concluded His sobering reminder with a promise, "...be of good cheer, for I have overcome the world." But as we look around, it can be hard to believe that our Lord has overcome. The world continues to plunge wildly on its errant way. Trouble proliferates and there are times when we simply cannot find the words. When the troubles deepen, and faith is under threat, we can turn to the Psalms.

The majority of the Psalms fall into the category of laments. There are two forms of laments in the Psalter, the individual lament and the communal. Together these Psalms comprise almost seventy percent of the Psalms. The majority of the Psalms speak out of the crucible of life's troubles. The form of these laments is familiar. They begin with an address to God, then the lament or complaint and finally an affirmation of trust in God's promises.

On many occasions, when my words have failed me, I have turned to the Psalms. They have given me Christ's overcoming strength in the midst of trouble. I know they can be a source of strength and comfort for you too.

Passion for God?

There is no shortage of passion and intensity around these days. In politics, the political maelstrom of the Middle East reflects a wider, global unrest that affects just about everything. Passion and intensity of the baser sort have found their way into nearly all expressions of the popular culture. I could go on, but you get the point. But what about God and His works and His ways? Are we passionate about them?

When his disciples saw Jesus turning over tables and giving money changers the lash, they got a good dose of passion and intensity alright. If any of us acted that way, we would call the cops and then look for a shrink to counsel us back into sanity. What came to the minds of the disciples when Jesus exploded in the Temple was a text from one of the Psalms: "Zeal for your house will consume me." Passion and intensity are what zeal is all about. And Jesus had plenty of it.

In the season of Lent, it is tempting to start in about how passionate and intense we should be where God is concerned. Really? Well, yes, but we passed the point of no return on that score so long ago it hardly bears mentioning. From what I can see we are passionate all right-passionate about everything but God.

Whatever little bit of interest, devotion and the like we can muster is fine, I suppose, but what captivates me about this story is that this Jesus, whose passion for righteousness and holiness shone like the sun, went to the Cross for the unrighteous and the unholy. He allowed us to put Him to death - us, about whom it could aptly be said, "Zeal for death consumes us."

So, as Lent wind's its way homeward, toward the Cross and the empty tomb, let's not make the story about our passion for God - please. Let us glory in the One whose zeal for righteousness and holiness is only matched by His love for sinners. Thanks be to God!

Demons

Modern people have trouble with the idea of demons. Demons seem so archaic, so primitive, so abstract. There is nothing abstract, however, about the man Jesus encountered as reported in Mark's gospel. Here we have the picture of a man driven to live in a graveyard. It seems others had tried to subdue him, even going to the extreme of putting him in chains but he was uncontrollable. So he ends up among the dead. A wild, dangerous creature who, Mark tells us, was given to hysteria and self-mutilation. Not very abstract.

Then Jesus shows up amid the death, screams and blood. This is just the sort of thing He is looking for. While everyone else stands around in their helplessness, Jesus acts. With a word, the demons are sent reeling and the man, now set free from his bondage, restored and basking in the Light of Christ, sees a new future open before him. He wants to go with Jesus but the Lord sends him home to tell of what God has done.

There will be more death, screams and blood in Jesus future. But this time the demons will be swirling around the Cross. The death will be His, the screams will be His, the blood will be His. Nothing very abstract here, either.

When Jesus died, so did you. Oh, you may be walking around taking breaths and putting a day together, but the fact is that His death put an end to your bondage also. The message of Jesus' Cross is not a kind of universal abstraction that is offered to your so-called free will to accept or reject. The Word of God is no abstraction just as our struggling, suffering willful lives are no abstraction. So, God shows up in His Gospel - the message of Cross and Resurrection - and puts our old selves to death, sets us free from our bondage to the powers that have driven us into the realms of death - our sinful self, the world and the Evil One. There is nothing left but simply to do as Jesus told the healed demoniac to do: "Go home to your own people and tell them how much the Lord has done for you, and how he has had mercy on you."

Concern? Yes. Worry? No.

Martin Luther once observed that birds lack faith. When he walked in the garden, they took flight though he meant them no harm. Fear is everywhere, and because it is, we spend significant amounts of our life's energies and resources in attempting to secure ourselves against real or perceived threats.

The disciples, caught in a storm on the Sea of Galilee, were beside themselves with panic. They rousted Jesus from his sleep, wondering if He was indifferent to the immediate danger. Our Lord Jesus saw things for what they were. Why were they afraid? Had the reality of faith still eluded them? Well, yes.

You can sense the concern in our Lord's questions. They were with Him. What was there to fear? And so it is for us. We belong to Jesus Christ. In Baptism He has promised to be our God, to go all the way with us through thick and thin. His faithfulness to us is what defines our relationship to Him. When we wring our hands in frustration, worry and fear over the myriad plights of life, we join the chorus of anxiety exemplified by the distraught disciples.

But the love of Jesus casts out fear, calms the anxious mind and holds us in the firm grip of grace. So, dear Christian, remember this, because of our sinful selves, the world and the Evil One there is much to be concerned about. But fear not! Because of Jesus Christ, there is nothing to worry about!

"Truly, truly, I say to you, he who hears My word, and believes Him who sent Me, has eternal life, and does not come into judgment, but has passed out of death into life." John 5:24

A couple had been attending worship on and off for several months when they met the pastor at the door following the service and announced that this would be their last Sunday. The pastor asked them why. The woman replied, "You Lutherans talk about sin so much. You're too negative. We found a church where they never mention it. It's much more positive."

I was not that pastor, but I have heard similar remarks over the years. And something I like to point out to those who make such comments is that the words 'positive' and 'negative' are nowhere in the Bible. Those are not the proper categories for biblical preaching nor do they adequately address the human predicament.

If positive and negative are not adequate categories for addressing our situation, what categories do we use? The Bible speaks of death and life. These are the terms that get to the heart of things. Any church that is not willing to deal with you on these terms is simply not taking you seriously.

The Christian message is not a religious self-help course, offering tips for living to those who need a bit more optimism or a more positive attitude. Christ Jesus has met us at the point of our deepest need, forgiving our sin, our willfulness and defeating death so that, in Him, we might have authentic life and a real future.

Many years ago, one of my seminary professors attended the funeral of the politician Hubert Humphrey. A famous TV preacher took to the pulpit and began to wax eloquently about Hubert's life. "Hubert never let things get him down", he said, "Hubert was always on the upswing, always positive." Prof. Kolden looked over at the casket and said to himself, "Well, Hubert, is that positive attitude of yours going to get you out of that casket?" Exactly.

"All flesh is grass and all its glory like the flower of grass. The grass withers, the flower fades, but the Word of the Lord abides forever." 1 Peter 1:24-25

For many, the bright flowers of the Easter festival quickly fade into the ordinary routines of daily living. What was observed was a day and nothing more.

But the real Easter endures. For what is Easter if not the promise of God's eternal victory in Jesus Christ, a victory that begins now in faith and is brought to perfection in the life to come?

The wedding service contains these words, "By your promises bind yourselves to one another...." Marriage begins with a promise and lives on that promise, "...until death parts us." Other aspects of life together may not stand the test of time; children, career, friendships, health may all fail us, but the promise is meant to endure. Sadly, for many, the promise also fails, withers, fades.

God's promise does not fail. "The Word of the Lord abides forever," proclaims the Scripture. Easter Sunday and every Sunday bear witness to the God who keeps his promises. This simple truth has been the bedrock of assurance for millions. It can be that for you, too.

"For the wages of sin is death, but the free gift of God is eternal life in Christ Jesus our Lord." Romans 6:23

I was speaking with a young physician following a funeral. He asked, "Why is death stronger than life? Why isn't it the other way around?" In response, I quoted the text above. We die because we sin. No matter how flourishing a life we may have lived, we all have sinned and death is our future. Pretty simple.

The inevitability of death can result in efforts to rationalize, to attempt to put a positive construction on death, to put the proper "spin" on death, and thereby diffuse it of its sting and power. We like to say things like, "Well, at least he didn't suffer"- if, in fact, that is the case. Or, "She had a long life and did everything she wanted to do," and so on. Or, keeping fashion with the latest in the rhetoric of death denial, nowadays you don't even die, you simply "pass." Whatever that means.

But can we really believe that these assessments are an adequate response to something that robs us of everything, including life itself? They sound much more like the remarks of those who are powerless and do notknow what to say in the face of the sobering and irrefutable truth that the world is a graveyard.

The Christian faith does know what to say. The Scriptures do not gloss over death and treat it like a minor bump in the road on our inevitable way to some spiritual never-never land. The culture may deny it, sanitize it, rationalize it, try to make the best of it and so on, but Saint Paul called it what it is: "The wages of sin." So I quoted St. Paul to the young doctor, who did not care much for what Saint Paul had to say about sin and death.

I also reminded him of the free gift. I told him that God in Jesus Christ has forgiven sin and defeated death on the Cross and that it is because Jesus lives that we may look forward in trust and hope to everlasting life. My young friend wasn't so sure about that either but he did concede that it was quite a promise. "Indeed it is", I replied, "and it is for you."

The Wedding Feast

Linda and I stepped out of the elevator and onto a rooftop restaurant that looks out on the ancient Roman Forum. The beautifully set tables announced that a gathering was imminent. And sure enough, after just a few minutes, every seat was filled. A large family and some friends were gathering after a First Communion. Wine began flowing, food was served. The setting was spectacular, the atmosphere joyful, full of life, a celebration. It was great to be there, even if we were on the outside looking in.

Thank God for these moments. Respites when we may gather with others for celebrations, brief truces in the wider conflicts and pressures of living, little glimpses of God's promised future.

When our Lord Jesus Christ gathered with His disciples for what we know as the Last Supper, He was giving them His last will and testament, His body and blood, the gifts of the Gospel. He also gave them, and us, a foretaste of the future. "I will not drink of the cup again," He said, "until I drink it with you in my Father's kingdom." In other places, Christ Jesus described the coming kingdom as a marriage feast that knows no end. In every service of Holy Communion the future comes to meet us, full of joy and promise.

Some day, we will all be gathered at the banquet of the Lamb. Fellowship with the Living God will be the occasion for us. The endless drone of the world's melancholy will finally give way to the joyous harmonies of eternal Easter, the glorious celebration that Christ has prepared for His people.

"Therefore, since we are surrounded by so great a cloud of witnesses, let us also lay aside every weight, and sin which clings so closely, and let us run with endurance the race that is set before us." Hebrews 12:1

To be sure, people were no better or worse in the "good ol' days" but when compared with today, many, many more children grew up in the midst of the strong, supportive structures of family, church and community.

For many young people today that world is largely gone. Families are scattered everywhere. Ours is no exception. Our immediate family members can be found in Wisconsin, Minnesota, New York, Washington, D.C. and Los Angeles. In such an environment it is not hard to understand the bewilderment of so many young people, their cynicism and uncertainty about the future. Where do they find an enduring set of values by which to order their lives, something worth living for?

When many young people look at the Church, the community that points to the magnetic figure of Jesus, they are often disillusioned by the time and energy poured into pursuing wealth and comfort by those who sit in the pews.

An old story tells of a young orphan boy who was taunted for his faith, "It seems your God has forgotten you," someone said to him. "No," he replied, "God has not forgotten me. But God's people have."

The Church has always been a place where the lost are found, where the hopeless find hope, where those disillusioned or crushed by the brokenness of their earthly families find the love and support of God's family. Not only are we surrounded by that great cloud of witnesses, cheering us on from the halls of heaven, we also have a role. People caught in the dislocation, alienation and mass estrangement of our time are searching for a place to stand, where an authentic life of faith, hope, and love is possible. The Church can be such a place.

"As each one has received a special gift, employ it in serving one another as good stewards of the manifold grace of God." 1 Peter 4:10

It took some doing, but after several miles on a hilly gravel road that wound past wineries and olive groves, Linda and I arrived at the Abbey of Sant' Antimo, nestled in a remote valley deep in the hills of Tuscany. The current church was commissioned in the 8th century, according to tradition, at the order of Charlemagne, the Holy Roman Emperor. Today, the stewards of this place are a small group of monks (the Canons Regular of the Augustinian Order) whose purpose is to engage in a ministry of worship for all who visit the church.

As a Lutheran Christian, I could not help but think back to Martin Luther's years as a monk. He was also an Augustinian but of a group called the Order of Hermits. He spent many years in that life, praying, studying, seeking solace and salvation. The monastic life was among the prescribed avenues through which, it was hoped, holiness could be developed and salvation finally achieved.

You probably know the story. Prescriptions for spiritual advancement and peace eluded him until, finally, he heard the promise of the Gospel: we are made right with God by faith alone, and not through our efforts, works or sincerity in cooperation with God. Christ alone is our righteousness. Our confidence is in Him alone. The new-found freedom that resulted led Luther from the self-conscious seclusion of monastic life to an open engagement with the world: marriage, children, community responsibilities, the struggle of reform.

In your baptism, Christ Jesus has called you to the vocation of living. Family life, occupational pursuits and the whole host of life's obligations and responsibilities are not secondary to what some call, "full-time Christian service." There are times in the life of every Christian when pulling back is necessary for prayer, reflection and renewal. But the Christian life is finally not one of retreat from life but engagement with life.

"For you were called to freedom, brethren; only do not use your freedom as an opportunity for the flesh, but through love be servants of one another." Galatians 5:13

"You can have it all," the saying goes. How many times and in how many ways has this promise been pushed at us from all corners of life? It is a false promise, of course, but one to which we are terribly vulnerable. Why? Partially because of our wants, or to put it a bit more forcefully, our appetites. And when our appetites for things, for experiences, for money, for security, etc, drive us we begin to see life as a quest for acquisition, for having what we want, for personal fulfillment. How many lives that have been shipwrecked in the pursuit of "having it all" is beyond calculating.

One area of life where the impact of this false promise has been devastating is the family. Raising children means setting your own fulfillment aside for the sake of the children. Parents may not recognize it, but such commitment is the key to their fulfillment. If a couple continues to defend their right to personal fulfillment after marriage they probably should not be parents. Their suitability for marriage itself may be called into question.

The basic problem with this false promise is the premise, what it says about life. A meaningful life does not begin with me and what I want. Service and assuming obligations are the basis for a meaningful life. "Having it all" is the fairy tale that seduces us into the subjective fantasy land of fulfillment on our terms. The more you seek it the more it will elude you.

Sadly, the "having it all" mentality can also find its way into churches, where a gospel of personal fulfillment replaces the faith and freedom of the Gospel. The Scriptures tell us that Jesus came among us to serve and not to be served. A reading of the gospels reveals the extraordinary power and freedom this kind of living produced. It is this liberating life of love and service that God wants for His children.

In Christ, we have been set free from the insatiable pursuit of the self. In this freedom is true fulfillment, which cannot be pursued for its own sake. When love and service become our aim, fulfillment is thrown in.

"For the Lord looks on the heart." 1 Samuel 16:7

The Israelites chose the tall, handsome Saul as their king. He turned out to be a disaster. God sees the heart. Sooner or later, we may also, but often it is too late.

The "heart" as used in the Bible refers to what we might call the whole person. That is what God cares about, the whole you. God sees all and still loves. The outward appearance is only a part of you and you know it. Sometimes the outer appearance is better than "you," sometimes it is worse. We are fooled by people when we only see part of them. But God is not fooled and God still loves.

God sees the whole person, the terrible potential for evil which we overlook in ourselves and tend to suspect in others. God also works to bring good from evil. This we often fail to see in others, for we love ourselves too much and our neighbors too little.

The gospel is the Good News that God is committed to us in Christ. God sees everything, yet remains firm in his grace and love. Honesty in this life does not mean wearing your heart on your sleeve at all times for all people. At the same time, we can dare to be honest with Christ Jesus. He knows us as we are and wants only our good. We can dare to trust Him with what He already knows, the good and the bad.

God Set Up a Cross

The ancient world was a vast field of magnificent temples. Only buildings bespeaking power, permanence and ultimate authority could adequately proclaim the mystery of divinity. The gods deserved nothing less, or so thought the ancients. Then God set up a Cross.

It was forged by nameless servants of imperial authority. A bare, rude thing. A time-tested instrument designed to evoke terror and coerce obedience through the application of unspeakable cruelty. Only the very worst, despised offenders suffered the fate of the crucified ones. The Romans lined roadways with them so that passers-by would be forced to carry the weight of pitiful suffering and inhale the stench of rotting corpses. It was about as far from divinity as one could get. This is the symbol of God's presence with us? Yes.

God set up His Cross where the four roads we travel most, meet: guilt, failure, spiritual poverty, and willful disobedience. The gift of God's Cross, the Baptism into Christ's death, is not given until I see that nothing in the world can address my sickness unto death except this one, impossible, ridiculous sacrifice. For only by the shame, cruelty and utter godlessness of the Cross can the true magnitude of our guilt and God's merciful love be measured. The message of the Cross proclaims to us what our true position in life really is. No wonder we flee from it for all we are worth.

Through Word and sacrament God continues to set up the Cross and the empty tomb in the center of our lives, and through them releases judgment and mercy, faith, hope and love. And since Christ Jesus embodies hope He rightly calls us to hope, not in our efforts, our so-called free will or determination, but in Him, the crucified. This is the scandal of the gospel. Jesus appears in the defenseless form of the crucified God to put an end to our pretensions to righteousness in order that we might have a righteousness based on faith. A righteousness won for us, the ungodly, through His death on the bloody Cross and His resurrection from the dead, where the true glory of God is revealed and where He wants to be known.

"Heal me " O Lord, and I will be healed; save me and I will be saved." Jeremiah 17:14

Pastoral ministry has exposed me to the debilitating presence of serious health issues in the lives of many. I have prayed with a mother of four in her thirties, stricken with cancer; the parents of a college freshman who came home on break only to fall into a coma with a fatally high fever; a young father with a list of health problems, any one of which would represent a significant challenge; and on and on it goes.

To suffer chronic illness or pain tries us to our limits. We may ask why. Perhaps we become bitter or resentful. We may even question God's grace and mercy. When I read the Scriptures, I see that God is on the side of life and health. Our Lord Jesus healed many during His earthly ministry. God's purpose was in those healings. Sickness and death are intruders in this world. We should not hesitate in praying for health and healing, trusting God's purpose for us.

At the same time, it is important to keep illness and healing in perspective. Even those who Jesus healed, including Lazarus who was raised from the grave, did not escape death. But sin and illness will not have the last word. God has promised that one day all this will be behind us. Until that Day death is the door through which we must enter the halls of eternity. No matter how many doctors or prayers we employ, this reality will not change. In this respect, pastoral experience has also permitted me to witness cheerfulness, patience, love and humor in many who struggle with debilitating illness.

So remember, even as you pray for God's healing presence and power, your witness to hope and grace in the midst of suffering can be one of the greatest gifts you give to those around you.

Our Shared Hopes

The cone-shaped objects hanging from the ceiling of a Vietnamese temple were spirals of burning incense. As Linda and I stood there, engulfed in the aromatic atmosphere, I could not help but reflect on how each one of these cones of incense represented someone's hopes and dreams. Some were prayers for dead ancestors, others for health, happiness, love and success, however defined. Some were certainly offered in gratitude. I was reminded of Christian traditions who also use incense as a symbol of their hopes and dreams offered in prayer. What is the difference?

In one very basic sense, there is little difference. Christians, like all people, look for fulfillment, meaning, value and redemption. You do not need to be a Christian to need or want these things. Some Christian people could afford to be far more charitable than they are toward their non-Christian neighbors who share the same hurts, hopes and longings.

Martin Luther once said that a Christian is a beggar who knows where the bread line is. That is about right. Who are we to look down our noses at non-Christians as if we did not share with them the same frail, needy humanity? If Christ Jesus, by His sheer grace and mercy, has opened your heart to see in Him the Father, it is not because of anything you have done. It is by His grace alone. If you have found the bread line, you are still a beggar.

So, as I stood there that day amidst the incense, I felt a kinship with those who were sending their hopes heavenward. And if I could I would tell each and every one of them that the crucified and risen Jesus is the face of the One who hears their prayers. I would invite them into the bread line to receive the Bread of Life. This is what we want to say to those who share our need for God.

"A cheerful heart is good medicine." Proverbs 17:22

"I don't know if I should laugh or cry." Have you ever expressed this sentiment? God has given human beings the gift of laughter. He has also enabled us to cry. To know when to laugh and to cry is a gift. In most cases, wherever possible, my vote is for laughter.

Much that passes as humor in today's popular culture is crude, cynical, taking delight either in the sufferings of others or in belittling others. This is not the Christian way.

People who can laugh at themselves take the world seriously but not too seriously. They are aware of the gap between what the world ought to be and the way it is, between what they ought to be and the way they are, but they do not give in to cynicism. This insight reaches deeply into our experience of life as people of faith. We are fallen creatures in a fallen world. The entire creation, including you and me, have been damaged by the presence of evil. We will always fall short of perfection, no matter how hard we try.

At times, if we have any sensitivity at all, we must grieve over this condition even to the point of shedding tears. That is appropriate. At the same time, Christians live in the light of God's grace and forgiveness. "Though your sins are like scarlet, I will make them white as snow," the Bible tells us. In Christ, God has closed the gap between what we ought to be and what we are. He declares us to be righteous in Christ, sees us as His sons and daughters.

To approach with humor the mishaps and problems of our lives and others with charity and good will can help lighten the load, if just a little, as we journey on toward the kingdom of joy that God has prepared for His people.

"... that you may have life in His name." John 20:31

It would not be inaccurate to characterize the verse above as the mission statement of John's gospel. John himself tells us that this is why he wrote, "...that you may have life in His name." "But I already have life,"'you may say. Perhaps.

God has arranged the world in such a way that we are able to invest ourselves in many modes of living and draw various dividends. We invest ourselves in marriage, and the results can be among the best in life: children, a loving partner, a home where we are nurtured and cared for. The joy of real friendships can add a dimension to our lives that nothing can replace. Meaningful work provides opportunity for service and fulfillment. The wide and variable richness of the world, our temporary home, provides a bounty of experience and resources for living.

But John does not present us with any of these. He does not send us back to ourselves, to others or to the creation to find life. We do not draw life, authentic life, from any of these, as good and beneficial as they may be. In fact, family, friendships, work and the creation itself can be the source of some of our greatest burdens, tragedies and sorrows. That is the way it is in a sinful world. The very things that we look to for life have a way of turning on us. They can take the life right out of us.

Jesus also found life in the things mentioned above. In the end, however, those same sinful forces that distort the good things in your life took His. But the Author of life is stronger than life-denying death. Christ is Risen!

So John brings you back to the very Source of your life, God Himself in Christ Jesus. In your Baptism, God promised to be and to remain the true source of your life through Christ so that when the lesser lights of life disappoint or are extinguished altogether, "you may have life in His name."

"The Son of Man came eating and drinking, and they say, 'Here is a glutton and a drunkard, a friend of tax collectors and sinners." Matthew 11:19

She sat in my church study, broken and defeated by life. Nothing had seemed to go right. Several failed marriages, legal problems and estrangement from her children were some of the burdens she was carrying. And all she could do was blame herself.

For a long time, she had tried to shut her eyes to the pain, the emptiness, and meaningless she felt, consoling herself in a life of frantic activity and day to day busyness which the world is always more than ready to provide for that purpose.

Now, she was convinced that God was punishing her. She doubted everything except her own worries, anxieties, fear and hopelessness.

In nearly four decades of ministry, I have known many like her. The problems vary, of course, as do the particular circumstances of living. Some have been rich, others of quite modest means. But what they have held in common has been a belief that God has dealt with them purely on the basis of sin and retribution. Perhaps you see something of yourself here, preoccupied with what has been lost, uncertain or even fearful as to God.

Jesus was called "friend of sinners" during His earthly life. The gospels report time and time again of His welcoming into His fellowship those who had lost themselves in sin. As time went on, it was these lost ones who became the greatest witnesses to His love.

When we look at ourselves, it is easy to become preoccupied with what has been lost. This is not hard to understand, since dealing with loss is a central theme in our lives. When God looks at you through Christ, however, He does not see what was lost, what you have squandered or mishandled. He sees only His child to whom He freely gives love and forgiveness in Christ. This is the heart of the Gospel.

" For Christ is the end of the law, that every one who has faith may be justified." Romans 10:4

A popular song of a bygone era was the Cole Porter tune, 'Don't Fence Me In,' sung by the famous western stars Roy Rogers and Dale Evans, among others. The title could serve as the motto for the old Adam and Eve in each of us.

Laws (fences) come in many forms. The sheer number of laws that govern various aspects of our lives is staggering. If you were to ask the various legislators at the federal, state and municipal levels for a rationale for the passing of these laws, the generic response would be, "For the public good." In principle, that is the case. The law is meant to restrain evil and promote the good. Laws are fences.

God uses law, all law, to put fences around human conduct. Even a casual reading of the Ten Commandment can reveal quite clearly that these laws are intended for our good. Yet there is hardly a one we have not broken down in thought, word or deed.

Under these circumstances, there is no hope of being justified before God on the basis of what we do, even if our generous self-assessments look pretty good! So, Christ Jesus has entered in, taking upon Himself our sin and fulfilling in Himself the perfect righteousness demanded of you. Christ is the end of the law for everyone who has faith. This most certainly does not mean that while we are in this life laws do not matter. The fences must be kept up, taken down and new ones erected, from time to time. Sinners like us must govern as well and as wisely as we can.

But our hope is not in staying within the fences, in behaving ourselves. There is no progress or merit in the Christian life to be gained by staying within the fences. We look to Christ Jesus alone as our righteousness before God. His actual death on the Cross brings an end to the accusing power of the law. In Him, we are free to serve our neighbors and care for the world (and its fences) even as we wait for the final coming of God's kingdom.

"For there is no other name..." Acts 4:12

I once was a guest at a social gathering and found myself standing with a group of people who were discussing God. Opinions were all over the map. Some were agnostics, not sure. Others took the atheist route. Others had vague notions of a god in nature or spirituality. The discussion was lively and friendly until someone asked me what I thought. "God is the One who raised Jesus from the dead," was my reply. Suddenly, things got very quiet. Then the objections began. I have known other Christians who have had similar encounters.

Christian faith ceases to be Christian if Jesus drops out of the proclamation, the sharing of the faith. We do not witness to a generic god that can be molded and shaped to fit our opinions, a god that is derived from our gray matter.

The Easter faith bears witness to the God who, through the Cross and Resurrection, has planted Himself in history. In Jesus, we are reconciled to the person of God, not an idea about God.

The witness to the resurrection will always raise eyebrows and prompt objections. That is to be expected in a creature that is, by nature, hostile to the Creator. At the same time, it is through this very same witness to the Cross and Resurrection of Jesus that God has chosen to create faith, to bring us to confess Jesus, to bring us, and hold us in a living relationship. And when vague notions about God, or belief in no God at all, give way to this confession of Jesus as Lord, the power of the Cross and Resurrection has done its work! Sinners are forgiven and set free to join the joyous chorus of confession, "God is the One who raised Jesus from the dead!"

Sin Boldly, but...

While waiting for a flight connection, I struck up a conversation with a young Roman Catholic priest. After a few minutes of conversation, upon learning that I was a Lutheran pastor, he asked me about Luther's quote, "Sin boldly." I filled him in on the remainder of Luther's comment: "...but believe in Christ more boldly still." His reply was, "Oh, I hadn't heard about that part."

On the surface, and taken out of context, Luther's comment sounds like a blank check for the old sinner in us to go nuts! But this is hardly what Luther intended.

Preoccupation with our sinfulness leads us away from the assurance we have in God's forgiveness. Luther knew this as well as anyone. So, his comment is a way of saying, live your life in Christ in the confidence of faith! Of course, we will sin. It is inevitable, because as long as we are in this mortal body sin remains with us. Do not be so preoccupied with yourself. Rather, be preoccupied with how great Christ is! He has forgiven your sins, past, present and future. That is the gospel of freedom in which Luther rejoiced...and you can too!

"For the Son of Man came to seek and to save the lost." Luke 19:10

During the late 1950's our family lived in Hawaii where my father served as an Air Force chaplain. Our home was in a beautiful setting in the mountains above Pearl Harbor. My friends and I spent hours exploring the sugar cane fields and tropical forest. It was all great fun, until one day two of us wandered into an area that was far beyond where we had ever gone. At first, it was exciting as we searched for something familiar. But before long our excitement turned to fear and panic. We were lost. We were alone. I can still remember how it felt.

The sense of being lost is part of life in this broken, sinful world and it comes in many forms. There are people who are truly alone and cut off from others, living lives of isolation. Many others live in the midst of family, friends and co-workers yet still feel lost and alone, adrift.

A few years ago one of the most popular programs on television was entitled, 'Lost.' It told the stories of a fictional group of people who had survived a crash-landing on a tropical island. I think the popularity of the program had a lot to do with the root concept of lostness. There is a deep sense of lostness in millions of people today. Many feel adrift in uncharted waters. Maybe you feel that way, too.

God knows that being born into this world does not mean we will feel at home, in the deepest sense. For being lost and adrift is the basic spiritual condition of man and woman. Jesus said, "I came to seek and to save the lost." In a real sense, this is God's mission statement, this is why Jesus came. You may feel lost and adrift these days for any number of reasons. But know this. The One who died on the Cross for you and was raised for you always has you on His radar. This does not mean you will never know the struggle or feel the isolation and loneliness that come with life in a sinful world. But it does mean that through all the circumstances of living you are being held in the grip of God's grace. You are not alone.

God's Foolishness

Science and reason have become the cornerstones of modern life. In fact, the voices of cold reason proclaim that this is all there is. Nothing is higher than man's reason. We are the masters of our own future. Hope is in our hands.

The voices of cold reason have also given rise to an aggressive atheism which continually attempts to debunk religious faith, and instead wants to tie the human future to, well, who knows what? Scientific progress? Evolution? Interplanetary colonization? Don't worry about it, though. By the time the evolutionary, utopian future finally gets here you and I will be dead and will have no share in it. Now, there is a hopeful thought!

Reason and curiosity about life have given humanity something to do from the very beginning. I suspect this is what God had in mind for us all along. Other creatures pretty much follow their unerring instincts. God gave us the capacity to do more. We uncover, explore, examine, investigate, test and theorize. The benefits and risks are enormous. The human gift of reason, with all its marvelous capabilities, untethered from the awareness that such reason is a gift of God, however, becomes a mechanism for evil with all the terrible consequences. But none are more terrible than to strip the human heart of its trust in God.

So, I for one am not going to cast criticism at those who manage to find a church door on Sunday, or any day, even against these relentless pressures of arrogance and godlessness that are all around and within us. For in the hearing of the message of the Cross and Resurrection of Jesus, authentic hope is released and may take hold of the heart. God is not impressed with the exertions of human reason. He is not going to play that game. He owes no explanation to the arrogance of reason. This foolish wisdom of God, as Saint Paul termed it, gives real hope to you and me. The Cross and Resurrection of Jesus have opened a real future. Life is going somewhere, and that somewhere is to God Himself.

Is God there for You?

Martin Luther once wrote, "The Lord is, indeed, everywhere; but is He there for you?"

Years ago, while on a road trip with my boys in the mountains of Colorado, we came upon a horrific accident. A tour bus had been zipping along on that beautiful summer day when it was ripped into a bloody wreck by a huge boulder that had dislodged from the hillside just above the roadway. Given realities such as this, whenever I hear someone talking of communing with God in nature, because God is everywhere, I shudder.

So, our Lord Jesus, who is, indeed everywhere, has given us something in which we may receive, in confidence, a gracious God. The water of Baptism, the bread and wine of the Lord's Supper are material substances from the natural world. Apart from God's promise that is all they are. But because Christ Jesus has attached Himself to these earthly elements, commanding that they be given, they become means by which His grace is given - "for you."

We may attend to these gifts in confidence, knowing that to receive the water of Baptism and the bread and the wine of the Lord's Supper is to receive all the gifts that Christ's death and resurrection have won for us; forgiveness of sins, life and salvation.

God is, indeed, everywhere. If we leave it at that, however, we might as well say God is nowhere. But when Christ Jesus says he is there "for you" in word and sacrament, it is a promise. You can count on it.

Holy Week

When Linda and I stood among the olive trees in the Garden of Gethsemane, we were struck by how little the scene had changed in twenty centuries. We recalled the account of our Lord's bitter tears in this place as He looked ahead to the suffering that awaited Him. Another story also came to mind, when Jesus sat on this hillside looking across at the great temple, reflecting on the faithlessness of the people. The Bible tells us all He could do was weep.

I am old enough to remember a day when God's people made time for Holy Week. Most businesses closed between noon and 3 PM on Good Friday (the traditional time of Jesus crucifixion) so people could attend worship, and many churches were full. During the week, sanctuaries were open for prayer and meditation. People stopped in at all times of the day to pray, to think, to reflect, to be with Jesus, to contemplate His passion, to give thanks, to bear witness to their faith.

Over the years, I have routinely seen one or two people make their way into the church during the week. A few more may make the pilgrimage that I do not see, but you get the idea. Today, this is a common story often told across our land.

It would be easy to complain about this, but all I can do is feel saddened, saddened to see Christian people whose hearts and minds are so conformed to the works and ways of the world that their response to the Great and Holy Week of our faith is studied indifference. This observation does not need to be defended. It simply needs to be said. Perhaps you, Christian, need to hear it.

Seen in the light of such casual neglect, the wonder of God's grace seems even more amazing. But has it not always been so? We do not deserve the blessed Jesus. We do not belong in the same world with Him. But deserving has no place in the equation of grace.

So, our dear Lord Jesus struggled through His tears on that hillside outside Jerusalem twenty centuries ago, got to His feet and shouldered the terrible Cross for the faithless, undeserving ones, for you and me.

"And when he entered the temple, the chief priests and the elders of the people came up to him as he was teaching, and said, '"By what authority are you doing these things, and who gave you this authority?"' Matthew 21:23

One of the slogans I recall from the 1960's was 'Question Authority.' Young people were encouraged to be skeptical of all forms of governance, all forms of authority. How much of this was sheer willfulness or genuine concern for the public welfare is a matter that can be debated. But there can be no doubt that authority matters, because those in whom authority is invested have power. In fact, much of the story of human history is the story of the struggle to establish authority and therefore the right to wield power, for good or for ill.

According to the gospel accounts, Jesus spent a portion of Holy Week teaching in the Jerusalem temple. The issue became one of authority. His triumphal entry into the city, together with His driving the money changers out of the temple, created a tense atmosphere. The religious leaders, who had been aware of Jesus for some time, were running out of patience. As Jesus is teaching they confront Him, questioning the basis of His words and actions.

At the end of the day, the question of Jesus' authority to do what he did and say what he said is of the utmost importance. If Jesus was just another religious figure teaching principles and godly wisdom, then He simply becomes one more subject for the school of religion, equivalent to the Buddah, Mohammed or any number of religious practitioners.

But if the authority of Jesus is rooted uniquely in the Living God, then what He said and did have ultimate authority, in the cosmos and in your life, whether you acknowledge it or not. This is what the Scriptures proclaim and this is what Christians have believed and confessed about Him from the very beginning.

By His authority, the Holy Spirit works through Word and sacrament, to keep you in the grip of His grace and forgiveness and align you continually toward the eternal future He has prepared for His people. We may need, from time to time, to question earthly authority. We never need question His.

"Then Jesus entered the temple and drove out all who were selling and buying in the temple, and he overturned the tables of the money-changers and the seats of those who sold doves. He said to them, 'It is written, "My house shall be called a house of prayer;" but you are making it a den of robbers.'" Matthew 21:12

Matthew recalls this dramatic scene as occurring the day after the Lord's triumphal entry into Jerusalem. In the Gospel of John, once they have gathered their wits in the wake of this event, the disciples recalled the words of the psalmist, "Zeal for Your house consumes me." The tensions are rising in Jerusalem and the Lord's days are numbered.

Nowadays we look askance at people who demonstrate this kind of reckless passion in the name of God. "After all", we say, "it is just religion and nothing to get excited about." If the Lord tried something like this today we would call 911 and have him locked up. Surely there must be something wrong with Him. With Him, or with us?

Could the psalmists words be yours or mine? When was the last time zeal (read, 'passion') for the things of God consumed us? Do we, indeed, live "by every word that proceeds from the mouth of God", or are we generally content with living by "bread alone?"

If the money changers in the temple were a den of robbers, then so are the rest of us. For "the earth is the Lord's" and we have stolen our existence from Him.

Once again, therefore, our dear Lord Jesus is on His own. If anyone is going to bring spiritual sobriety to the human race it will have to be God Himself. We are too busy staying drunk on the things of this world, inebriated by the myriad seductions of life. So Jesus presses on toward His fate. The reason for His unwavering determination is simple: mercy and love. Jesus willingness to endure suffering and death was not the misguided mission of a religious madman. He endured it because of love, God's love-for you.

"If anyone comes to me and does not hate his father and mother, his wife and children, his brothers and sisters--yes, even his own life--he cannot be my disciple." Luke 14:26

Ouch! What are we supposed to make of words like these?

We make great projects out of our families. In our neighborhood, many have the financial resources to give their kids every possible advantage. As a parent, I can understand. Parents who care about their kids want what is best for them. Of course, this does beg the question, "What do we mean by best"?

In a culture where experience is a high value, some would interpret best to mean exposing kids to as many experiences as possible. Sports, travel, etc. What is best for kids, some say, is to keep kids busy.

Others see in the term 'best' the primacy of a good education. Today, companies exist to provide tutorial assistance to otherwise competent students. Why? To assist them in gaining an advantage in the competition for the best schools. What is 'best' is positioning your kids for a good education which will translate into a good career, financial security, etc.

There is nothing inherently wrong with any of this, I suppose. At the same time, if God is not in the picture, then the most intimate interpersonal relationships in life are what matter most. My kids matter most. In this respect, for unbelieving parents to make an idol out of the family is not surprising. There is nothing else of any higher value to worship.

But for Christian families, it is another story. What is 'best' for kids in Christian families is that they learn from their parents that no person in life or experience in life is more important than Jesus Christ and no task more important than nurturing faith in Him. If Christian parents can move heaven and earth to get their kids to the soccer field on Sunday mornings while ignoring the call to worship, perhaps the Lord's strong words need to be heard.

Jesus' words exclude all alternatives that would displace faith in Him, including the family and its priorities (whether we have children or not) because He wants His grace and mercy to be life's sure foundation. The Lord's words are tough. Sometimes love has to be.

143

God the First and God the Last

I was channel surfing one evening and came across a well-known television preacher. His topic was, more or less, why life does not work and what you can do about it. As to why life does not work, he suggested that it is because we are not in God's will. As to what we can do about it, he suggested what he identified as the Bible's blueprint for living. His message was that if we get life organized according to God's blueprint, life will work. And his version of God's blueprint looked like this:

First, God.

Second, family.

Third, others.

Fourth, self.

Sounds good, huh? Not so much. The problem here is that our T.V. friend has the wrong blueprint for the life of faith. Religion? Maybe. But not faith. This hierarchy of values approach to the Christian life is nothing more than the law packaged for those inclined toward self-help. It is an invitation to a project of endless self-improvement. Trying to reorganize your life around this scheme may help clarify your values, but it will not result in faith. And faith is what the Christian life is all about. So, let me suggest an authentic Biblical blueprint for living. It looks like this: God the first and God the last in everything.

Faith does not look to some idealized blueprint. The God we know in Jesus Christ does not sit at the top of a pyramid of diminishing values, waiting for us to engage our so-called free will in order to make everything work as you struggle to conform your life to some impossible ideal. Instead, trust in Christ and Him alone.For He is at work for you, anchoring you in Himself and in His promises, especially in the word of the Gospel proclaimed to you and the sacraments given for you. Christ Jesus is creating faith in you that looks to Him to be the Alpha and the Omega, the beginning and the end of all things. Such faith takes hold of life with a joyful daring, confident that His goodness is at work in every area of life.

"Love your neighbor as yourself." Love does no harm to a neighbor. Therefore love is the fulfillment of the law. " Romans 13:8

I would rather have rules. So would you. And it is not just civil society that advocates rules. Even the most criminal of organizations have just that, organization. We are all familiar with the dynamics of the mafia. Strict codes apply to every member. The rules must be followed. Living outside the rules is not to be tolerated.

The Pharisees of Jesus' day were what we might call the law and order folks. They were very much concerned with the orderly conduct of society, as you may be. They were not libertine, willful people who equated freedom with license to do as they pleased, as some of you may do. They recognized that living outside the law posed a risk not only to the person who did so, but also to society as a whole. This was certainly in the mind of the high priest at the trial of Jesus, when he declared that it was better that one person die than the whole people perish. The apparent lawlessness of Jesus might spread like a virus.

There has always been something of the Pharisee in the Church. Most comfortable, middle class congregations nod approvingly at the Bible's call to love sinners, until the sinners show up on the doorstep. This was the thrust of Jesus' parable of the Prodigal Son. The older brother was outraged that his younger, whore loving, money squandering brother who brought shame on the family, was welcomed back with open arms by the love of his father.

Love does not live outside the rules, it lives beyond the rules. To live beyond the rules is to recognize that love is the fulfillment of every rule, every law. This is the frightening, unknown territory where faith lives. The law and order folks, in the world and in too many churches, fear this territory and are reluctant to go there. But Jesus was not and is not afraid to go there. And if you claim Him as your own, the freedom he has won for you at the cost of His life, is on your hands. It is a frightening gift, to be sure. But faith has no other territory in which to establish itself. You may remain in the land of dead certainties or you may venture into the frightening freedom of faith, as our Lord did, where love knows no boundaries.

Reformation

I arrived in a congregation to begin my work as associate pastor for youth and parish education. On the first day of seventh grade confirmation class, I distributed a brief, one page set of questions to the kids in order to get a sense of their knowledge of the Bible and their Lutheran faith. One of the questions was, "Who was Martin Luther?" Well over half the class identified Martin Luther as a black man who was killed or had something to do with civil rights. A number of the kids answered that they did not know. Of that group of over twenty kids, three were able to identify Luther as the reformer.

At about the same time I was asked to address a large Sunday morning adult class on the subject of Luther. To begin, I described the theology of the Cross and the theology of glory and asked the group for a show of hands regarding which they thought represented Martin Luther's theology. Nearly every person went with the theology of glory. Wrong. No wonder the kids were clueless. I went home that morning in a blue funk. Not because I was surprised, but precisely because I had come to expect this.

Now, I am all for dusting off the 16th century once in a while and re-visiting the events of Luther's life and time. It is important to do so. At the same time, I am more concerned that people today who inhabit the corridors of Lutheran churches, or any church for that matter, have some inkling as to why Luther matters. Because he does.

And he matters not because Martin Luther got everything right but because he points us to what is essential, he points us to the Cross, to Christ where our true salvation is found. Luther read his Bible and there discovered that we have no right or need to say anything or do anything for our salvation. As far as God is concerned, we have nothing to offer. And it is pointless to climb religious ladders in search of glory. Rather, as beggars in the bread line we can do no other than hold out our empty hands and receive the salvation that God gives on His terms, by grace alone, in the crucified and risen Jesus.

"I am the gate; if anyone enters by me he will be saved and will go in and out and find pasture." John 10:9

Ancient sheep pens had only one gate. At night, when the sheep were gathered within the enclosure, the shepherd actually slept in the opening. He was there to keep the sheep from wandering off and to protect them from predators.

The writer of the Letter to the Ephesians gives us some perspective on the one Gate who is Christ, the Word of God. "There is one body and one Spirit, just as you were called to the one hope that belongs to your call, one Lord, one faith, one Baptism." (Ephesians 4:4-5)

The image of Jesus Christ as the Gate, the place of access, is focused, narrow and exclusive. It is meant to be. For it is only in the Word and promise of God through which the Holy Spirit unites us with the One Lord, into the One Faith, through the One Baptism. God in His gracious love not only tells us in His Word about what He has done for our salvation, but in the One Baptism He places the seal of promise upon our heads. In Baptism God, the Gate, opens the way, becomes the Way. In the One baptism God says, "Everything my Son has done is for you, not just for the world in general." In the One Baptism God makes the promise specific to you.

There is nothing flattering about Christ referring to us as sheep. It is an image of a creature who becomes easily lost, is vulnerable to predators and cannot look out for its own welfare. But because we are blessed to have a Good Shepherd, One who loves us and has given His life for us, we may enter the dicey business of living with confidence and assurance.

He who has called you by name in your Baptism and watches your going out and your coming in has opened your future. You can trust Him. For even this day He is leading you into the safety, abundance and freedom of His kingdom.

"Love does no wrong to a neighbor; therefore love is the fulfillment of the law." Romans 13:10

The first major storm of the hurricane season came on shore near New Orleans. Unwelcome flood waters drove many from their homes. News reporters stood in the withering downpours, like battlefield journalists, giving blow by blow descriptions of the storm and its progress. They brought us live pictures of driving rain, devastating winds and the valiant efforts of people as they struggled to stand against the onslaught.

We are also in another storm of sorts. It is has far more power than many hurricanes, inflicts untold amounts of damage and roars through the world virtually unchecked. That storm is the willfulness and assertion of the unrestrained self.

Self-indulgence and unfettered self-expression have become politically correct, even 'chic'. But this storm of self-expression wreaks havoc on all areas of life.

Christian people are called to stand against the maelstrom of human willfulness. And this begins with the self. At times, this requires from me a return to the diminutive, to repentance. It may also require me to support the application of human law in defense of society and its interests.

At all times the Christian is called to stand against the chaotic forces within life with the law of love. This is the God-given place of tranquility within the eye of the storm. This law is always defining for us and seeks to do no harm to the self or the neighbor. As Saint Paul has reminded us,

"Love is patient and kind; love does not envy or boast; it is not arrogant or rude. It does not insist on its own way; it is not irritable or resentful, it does not rejoice at wrongdoing, but rejoices with the truth. Love bears all things, believes all things, hopes all things, endures all things."

"Lord, will you at this time restore the kingdom to David?" Acts 1:6

The Lord's disciples wondered aloud if He had come to restore the kingdom of David. Jesus was dismayed and said, "Have I been with you so long and you still don't understand?" The mother of James and John asked the Lord that her two boys might have positions of honor and authority in His new kingdom. Jesus retorted that she had no idea what she was asking. Pontius Pilate asked if Jesus was a king. He replied, yes, except His kingdom was not of this world. On the day of the Ascension, as Jesus was taken up to heaven, the disciples were still asking, "Lord, will you at this time restore the kingdom to David?" They did not get it.

The push and pull of politics is as old as dirt-and at times worth about as much. It is not that we can dispense with politics, with earthly governance. All forms of governance are expressions of law. Some forms are better than others, but all have their temporary place in the management of human affairs. Power is at stake, of course. And wherever power is at stake, expect it to bring out the worst in people. Look again at the disciples. My suspicion is that all this high-minded talk about the kingdom of David had something to do with political payback, gaining the high ground, sticking it to the Romans. The blatant political self-interest of the mother of James and John was so embarrassingly obvious, Jesus waived it aside with a word.

Jesus did not come to establish an earthly kingdom. You would never know it, however, when you listen to many Christian voices - on the left and right - who claim to speak for God. While we wait for the new heaven and the new earth we must still live here. But this transitory life, so full of difficulty and conflict, can cause the Christian to lose sight of the goal and be consumed by the passions of politics. So we need to hear again how Jesus responded to these misplaced passions among His own.

"Who is this that forgives sins?" Luke 7:49

If a best friend lets you down, betrays your trust, your relationship is of a different character than it was before. Probably all of us at one time or another have been on one side of these dynamics or the other. Humanly speaking, we do not seem to have the emotional equipment to deal with faithlessness.

Now let us invite Jesus into the picture. He not only dealt with faithless people, He also spoke about forgiveness in a different way than anybody else. The people of His day were amazed at things He said, and they asked, "Who is this that forgives sins?"

Jesus not only forgave the sins of strangers that were considered unforgivable, He also forgave His best friends when they proved faithless. They had glorious opportunities to stand up and be counted as His friends. But they let Him down.

There is an old legend that tells of Jesus meeting Satan out in the desert just prior to His Ascension into heaven. Satan mocked the Lord for being so foolish as to think that His faithless followers would ever make it without His visible presence among them. The Lord replied that His disciples would trust Him and go out into the world in His name. Satan just laughed.

As it turned out, every one of His disciples, after Judas, was faithful unto death. They were faithful because their Lord forgave their faithlessness and remembered their sins no more.

The disciples went on to do glorious things in Christ's name. Do you think of yourself as too ordinary, too faithless to be of much good for Christ? Your lack of faith is not the story. He is always faithful. He not only forgives your sins, He forgets them. Do not be surprised if you find yourself with glorious opportunities to serve Him. In Baptism He has chosen you. The promise of His forgiveness makes all things new. You and I will remain ordinary and often faithless followers. But take heart, for we have an extraordinary and faithful Lord!

Let us rejoice and be glad and give him glory! For the wedding of the Lamb has come, and his bride has made herself ready."
Revelation 19:7

I have sat with engaged couples over the years who had begun to question their intention to marry. They were usually dismayed at this, but my counsel to them was that this is what engagement periods are for. An engagement period is supposed to be a time of searching and testing, a step toward the public promises of marriage. It is not the time of fulfillment and it may be the time that leads to the decision to go separate ways.

The important thing in this period of their life is that they learn to be faithful to one another. The time of engagement is the time of learning to trust. There is hope and love, too. But it is not until marriage that they discover that the "greatest of these is love."

So now in this life we live in faith and hope. Our love is immature. But when Christ Jesus comes again, when the Bridegroom comes to claim His bride, we will experience the full depth of His perfect love and realize why our faith and hope were not in vain. Christ's presence will be overwhelming, His purpose so obvious, His love so completely satisfying, that all doubts will be stilled and all longings fulfilled.

"So we do not lose heart. Even though our outer nature is wasting away, our inner nature is being renewed day by day. For this slight momentary affliction is preparing us for an eternal weight of glory beyond all measure, because we look not at what can be seen but at what cannot be seen; for what can be seen is temporary, but what cannot be seen is eternal." 2 Corinthians 4:16-18

Located in the ancient Greek city of Olympia is a ruined structure that was once the workshop of Phidias, the greatest sculptor of classical antiquity. Among his many works were the statue of the Olympian Zeus, one of the seven wonders of the ancient world, and the statue of Athena which stood in the Parthenon of Athens. None of the splendid works of Phidias have survived. His work is only known from a few Roman copies and images on coins. One of the greatest bodies of artistic work ever produced is simply gone.

The sobering lessons of history can be hard to learn. For all our blustering and stamping about on this tiny, celestial ball the fact remains we are mortal creatures in a temporal existence. Human workmanship, even at its most glorious, eventually goes to dust and so do we. Nothing we put our hands to will stand the test of time. This does not have to be defended but it does need to be said.

The work of restoration that was begun 2,000 years ago at the Cross of Christ is contemporaneous with our lives today. For even as the produce of human history is perpetually plowed back into the earth, the renewing, saving Word of the Gospel continues to create new people in Christ. The temporal consequences of the human story lead to a dead-end future. The eternal consequences of God's work lead to an eternal future where what He has created in Christ Jesus will remain, pure and undefiled forever.

"Looking to Jesus the pioneer and perfecter of our faith, who for the joy that was set before him, endured the Cross, despising the shame, and is seated at the right hand of the throne of God." Hebrews 12:2

Every day our noses are rubbed in the calamities and arguments playing out on the world stage. Closer to home the brittle conflicts in our own society are driving people farther apart as the melting pot boils over in rancor and mistrust. Our personal lives struggle with faltering financial assumptions and the pressures and stresses of a too rapidly changing, even chaotic life. The current state of affairs brings forth a question: dare we be joyful?

I am not referring here to those experiences or possessions with which we temporarily maroon ourselves from the world and its troubles: happiness, pleasures, having fun or good times. These, after all, are not synonymous with joy. The use of joy within the Christian family is something different.

When the Scriptures refer to joy it is always to be understood in relation to God. But are we speaking here of an invitation to or an imperative to enter a kind of monastic life where we may escape the seething, hurting world, and have a life of meditation and prayer with God where we achieve a kind of inner tranquility and joy? Is that what our Lord wants?

Writing from his imprisonment in Rome, Saint Paul encouraged the Philippian congregation to "Rejoice in the Lord always." There must be on the part of God a hope, an invitation, even a command to be joyful in the fact that he has come to us in Christ Jesus.

The joy of the Christian is in God Himself. Saint Paul could write joyfully from his imprisonment because his consciousness of the Lord was greater than his self-consciousness. He would not treat his sufferings as if they were greater than his Lord.

"For God so loved the world, He gave His only Son..." John 3:16

I was chatting with a woman in line at the grocery store who, upon learning I was a pastor, made the statement, "I'm very spiritual and religious but I don't go to church." She spoke quite generally about some sort of god and spirit and feeling and nature. I replied by saying that although a pastor, I was not very spiritual or religious. She was rather surprised at this. "Then what do you talk about?", she asked. "Jesus", I answered. "Everything we are looking for in what we call religion and spirituality are found in Jesus Christ." Before she could respond it was time to check out. As she pushed her cart away she looked back at me with a slight smile and a somewhat puzzled expression. I considered it a good days work!

The essence of the Christian message is this: "For God so loved the world, He gave His only Son." This ought to be good news to serious seekers after God. The fact that it is not calls into question just how serious all this talk about seeking God really is. Some sort of god on my terms perhaps, but the True God? I'm not so sure.

God has taken the guesswork out of religion and spirituality and has revealed Himself with pinpoint accuracy in Jesus of Nazareth. Jesus is the human face of God. What Jesus says and does are the words and deeds of God. Read the gospels. See for yourself. Here is a man passionate about justice, set firmly against evil, eager to be with the outclassed and the outcast, available to all, full of grace, determined to make all things new, brimming over with truth, so much a part of God they are one, big enough to carry suffering, even death, so committed in love to the sinner that even death could not hold Him. What is not to like?

So, you can have a vague spirituality cobbled together out of, well, whatever. Or you can have Jesus. Friend of sinners, Prince of Peace, the Living Water, the Bread of Life, the Good Shepherd. I could go on but you get the point. There is nothing vague about Jesus. The faith, hope, love, grace, judgment, mercy and forgiveness that are in Him are as real and refreshing as rain. And they are for you!

"I can do all things through Christ who strengthens me."
Philippians 4:13

The impacted and chaotic character of the modern world reflects forces that are akin to the principalities and powers of which the New Testament speaks. They are on the loose and on our hands. It seems we are left to ourselves to invent ways to describe and attempt some kind of control of events and the forces that are their causes. This self-management project brings mixed results, to say the least.

Jesus said to His disciples, "Apart from me you can do nothing." This was not exactly a ringing endorsement of humanity's competency apart from God. It is a flat statement of a sobering truth. The human project, broken from its' moorings to the Living God, will inevitably be shipwrecked. This is among the clearest lessons of history. But it's only part of the story.

The one who made this statement, pointing out our powerlessness, is also the one who has committed Himself to us in love, who gave Himself on the Cross and was raised for our justification. Knowing this, Saint Paul could say, "I can do all things through Christ who strengthens me." The Christian life is proactive because it is rooted in the God who "seeks and saves the lost." All the verbs in the New Testament which describe the activity of the Church and the individual Christian, have one subject: God in Christ working through the Holy Spirit.

Apart from this God, the world and the Church have no prospects. With Him, all things are possible and a gracious, hopeful future is assured.

"This is the day the LORD has made; let us rejoice and be glad in it." Psalm 118:24

The Ponte Rotto is one of the most ancient bridges in Rome, and the first stone bridge erected there by the Roman engineers. Today, one large section remains, detached from either shore, marooned in the center of the Tiber.

As Linda and I stood there pondering this antiquated rock pile the words of a song came to my mind. "The past is past and tomorrow is not here-only what we do for Jesus today will last." It's not the best of lyrics but it does carry a point. Yesterday is gone and no retrieval of its opportunities is possible. Yesterday has been written and the ink is dry. Tomorrow is yet to be. I assume it will come but it may not. I may not lean forward to catch a glimpse, nor does a hint of tomorrow come like the first blush of sunrise, long before the rising.

God has designed our lives in such a way that we live in the present moment. Really, faith is not possible under any other circumstance. I am called to entrust my past to God, to believe that it has been carried up into His forgiveness. In a similar way I entrust tomorrow to God's purpose and look forward in hope. Both directions are inaccessible to me as I live between the already and the not yet.

So here we are at the threshold of a new and untried day. Like someone peering out from the vantage point of that ancient bridge, we have one option, to breathe in the moment and take hold of this day. For people of faith today is enough.

On that October morning in Rome as we stood gazing at the day unfolding around us, another lyric came to mind, that of the Psalmist: "This is the day the Lord has made. Let us rejoice and be glad in it."

"How, then, can they call on the one they have not believed in? And how can they believe in the one of whom they have not heard? And how can they hear without someone preaching to them?" Romans 10:14

A pastor was showing a good friend around the sanctuary of his church. It was a beautiful, gothic style building constructed in the 19th century. When they came to the large round pulpit the visitor saw that access to the pulpit was through a locked doorway. The pastor commented that over the years the pastor of the congregation was the only one permitted to have a key.

"The pulpit is for Christ and His gospel," the pastor said. "The congregation does not want someone wasting their time by using the pulpit to give opinions or lectures or tips for living. No one preaches here unless they preach Christ."

Today, some, perhaps many, would label him and that congregation intolerant, lacking an inclusive spirit. In a time of widespread confusion over the nature of the Christian message many in the Church prefer a sort of shotgun approach to truth. Just blast away with as many opinions as possible and somehow, somewhere, the truth just may show up.

There was a time in our Lutheran tradition when laity paid scrupulous attention to the preached Word. They knew what to listen for as Gods' Law and Gospel were proclaimed. They were not afraid to confront the preacher if he veered off into opinions and speculations. Giving the pastor the key to the pulpit, after all, represents a careful management of God's Word that is the responsibility of the whole congregation. We entrust our pastors with the task of regular preaching. At the same time, laity have an obligation to keep their pastors on point. Not as an expression of intolerance, but as an expression of their commitment to see to it, as the Lutheran Confessions declare, that "the Gospel is proclaimed in its purity." The message of the forgiveness of sins, life and salvation that are in Jesus Christ depend upon it.

"I am with you always." Matthew 28:20

During my seminary years we worshiped at a Lutheran church located directly across the street from the campus. Other regular worshipers were Dr. Alvin Rogness, former president of the seminary, and his wife, Nora. We often sat together during the service and visited during the fellowship hour.

Al and Nora lost a son to a tragic accident some years before. The young man was returning home from a year of study at Oxford. At the airport in Minneapolis, ten minutes from home, but accustomed to the flow of English traffic, he stepped off the curb and looked the wrong way. A truck ran over him.

One Sunday morning after worship Al and Nora spoke of those early days of grief and shock. People brought condolences, but words did little. Al recalled looking out the window of their home one day shortly after their son died only to see a friend from out of town walking up the street to their home. He had heard the news and came as soon as he could. Just seeing him, Al said, was the best comfort they could receive. What meant the most was people's presence. Nothing needed to be said.

After many years of being with the grieving, I know what Al and Nora observed is true. I have seen many mourners at funerals and gravesides who never spoke a word but expressed their love, sorrow and comfort with their tears, a touch on the hand or a warm embrace. There is simply no substitute for being there.

"I am with you always," the Lord promised his disciples. Christ Jesus gives us this promise of His presence in the midst of all forms of living and dying. For there are times when the Christian has no option but to sink into grief over the relentless sorrows of the confounding world. At such times we may find ourselves unable to hear even the words of our faith. At such times, as in all times, His presence brings that peace and comfort the world neither knows nor gives.

"Let us give thanks to the God and Father of our Lord Jesus Christ! For in our union with Christ he has blessed us by giving us every spiritual blessing in the heavenly places. Even before the world was made, God had already chosen us to be his through our union with Christ, so that we might be holy and blameless before him." 1 Peter 1:3-7

My rock n' roll years were spent as a teenager in southern California. I had the privilege of playing in a band managed by the well-known disc jockey, Casey Kasem. He was famous for a statement he used at the end of his long running radio and TV programs. You might remember it.

"Keep your feet on the ground and keep reaching for the stars."

The world has a way of keeping our feet on the ground and our noses in the dirt. Created for the heavens, we too often find ourselves choking on the dust, immersed in the tedium and coarseness of life. On the one hand, of course, we have no choice. We must live in this world and be real about it. But there is more.

Saint Paul begins his letter to the Ephesian Christians by turning their sights from the earth to the stars. In these two verses from the beginning of his letter he describes a great mystery, a mystery of which we are a part as God's people. We are thankful for the great opportunity of our lives, of course. At the same time it is our life in Christ Jesus, our life in God that draws from the Christian the greatest swell of thanks and praise. How can we fathom it? All the blessings of heaven, Paul, declares, are already ours in Christ. Before the dawn of time, of creation, Paul tells us, God had already chosen us as His own through Christ. And right there, within the great mystery of predestination, of election, emanating from God's eternal, steadfast love, the greatest mystery of all was present and waiting to be revealed.

And what is that most ineffable of mysteries? That on the earth-bound, bloody cross the dear, holy, blessed, heavenly Jesus became sin although He knew no sin so that our sinful selves would be overwhelmed by the grace and mercy of the eternal God, and "that we might be holy and blameless before Him." Thanks be to God!

159

Confessing Creeds

The historic creeds have enduring value. Here is why I believe this to be true.

First, the creeds remind us that the Church is far more than a group of like-minded individuals. The creeds point the Church to what God has done for the salvation of the world. They are not, first and foremost, expressions of personal piety. The creeds point us to events, to the mighty acts of God. In this respect the creeds are objective statements fit for every time and place.

Second, the ongoing confession of the creeds are like the links of a chain which bind Christians to the historical continuity of the Church. The radical, sectarian elements in the Church who disavow the creeds and discount their connection with the wider Church, run the risk of losing the faith itself. The creeds bind us to one another in a common confession across the generations.

Third, the creeds are Biblical. That is to say, they reflect the faith proclaimed in the Scriptures. In this respect, they are not man-made as some would claim. The language of the creeds is drawn from Holy Scripture and, therefore, that same language invites us to examine the Scriptures. The creeds send us to Scripture and, ultimately, to Jesus Christ.

Fourth, the creeds provide the individual believer with language rooted deeply in the Gospel, language which must be continually unfolded and re-examined so that our individual and corporate confession of faith may be made with an honesty and integrity rooted both in the Church's long history and the demands of the present.

In a sermon from 1535 Martin Luther commented on the Apostle's creed with these words. "Neither we nor the early fathers invented this confession of faith, but just as a bee collects honey from all kinds of beautiful flowers so is the Apostle's Creed a finely constructed summary of the whole of Scripture, the writings of the beloved prophets and apostles, for the benefit of children and all Christians."

"I believe in God the Father Almighty"

To confess God as Father is to identify with the God of Jesus. Some today refuse to use the word 'Father' when speaking of God. They reject the word for reasons largely shaped by issues of gender. But can the word be dismissed so arbitrarily? We confess God as Father not because it is the only word but because it is the word Jesus used. It is the word of the Bible.

To confess God as Almighty is to say something about how God is encountered in history, in our lives. The pagan religions of the Old Testament saw the power of gods revealed in the finite: the sun, the moon, the stars, etc. The God of Israel, on the other hand, was perceived to be active in the midst of what we call historical events in surprising, unexpected ways. God's activity could come as bondage or freedom, destruction or salvation. Israel's faith emerged in this dynamic, as what became most real to them were the recurring acts of God's mercy in their restoration and salvation. For now, I must confess in faith this God Almighty who kills and makes alive in His mercy, since the final coming and revealing of His Almighty power lies in the future.

In confessing God as Father Almighty, we are led to see Jesus in the light of God's saving activity as a personal God, active in our lives with a redemptive purpose.

Jesus is Lord

Belief in God runs off in as many directions as there are those who make such a confession. Even to confess belief in a God of creation does not really say much. As Martin Luther observed, "God may be in the creation, but is He there for you?" How does this God meet us in the precarious historical situation in which we find ourselves in this world, surrounded as we are by powers too great for us, especially death?

The Christian confession of the God of creation finds its center in Jesus, who we call the Christ, Messiah, Savior. In making this confession the Church is saying that the historical life of Jesus of Nazareth was the radically singular event in God's self-revelation and the history of the world. Jesus' words and actions were the words and actions of the self-expressing God who was "in Christ reconciling the world to Himself." To confess "... Jesus Christ, His only Son..." is to say that God and Jesus may be mutually substituted for one another and that they really include one another. Therefore, Jesus is not an open question who points humanity to God. In Jesus God responds to the questions posed by our radically fallen existence fully and unconditionally.

In Jesus, God reveals His saving divine will and grace for the sake of a humanity that is derivative of this same Jesus, the Word made flesh. "All things were made through Him and without Him was not anything made that was made." The confession of faith in this Jesus which calls Him "...our Lord," is an acknowledgment of trust in the One who alone has the absolute right to judge our lives and demand the radical self-surrender of man and woman, in faith, to the Word of God. This self-surrender, however, is brought about by grace. Whoever is able to make this confession does so by grace ("No one can say Jesus is Lord, except by the Holy Spirit"). But this grace is not a divine substance given to assist us in loving. Grace is God Himself, giving Himself in love, fully and completely for us.

To call Jesus Lord is to confess, therefore, that in Him, the crucified and risen One, God has given Himself unconditionally for sinful humanity. And that through this faith, I may look forward in hope to the fulfillment of the final possibility of God's saving purpose.

"And in Jesus Christ, His only Son, our Lord..."

The section of the Apostle's Creed dealing with Jesus Christ is as significant for what it does not say as it is for what it says. Missing from this section of the creed is any reference to the teachings and works of Jesus. The language moves from His birth immediately to His death, resurrection and the events following, including His Ascension to the Father. This pattern is present in all the ancient creeds of the Church. Therefore, it is not accidental.

What is mentioned was of the greatest significance to the early Church. The details of the Christological section of the creed provide the basis and criterion for understanding and confessing what is essential about Jesus and His Gospel.

In this article of the creed "crucified" appears with the words "suffered", "died" and "buried". One would think a reference to crucifixion would be superfluous under the circumstances. Why this specific reference to the manner of Jesus' death?

The answer, I believe, lies in the fact that the event of the cross is the key to understanding the meaning of Jesus entire mission to this world. On the cross, humanity looked upon the One who had encountered them in love and righteousness and dealt with him as a common criminal. The event of the cross, then, exposes human antipathy toward the Living God and puts the lie to all our claims to love justice.

The event of the crucifixion is mentioned in the creed because this event, unlike any other in all of history, confronts men and women with the enormity of our crime; the theft of our existence and contempt for the Living God. At the same time the cross reveals God's intention to have mercy on us. The Cross of Jesus is the consequence of God's love. On the cross God reveals His intention to make an end of all that we do, for all that we do is finally unsustainable and leads to death.

"God is not mocked, for whatever a man sows, that he will also reap." Galatians 6:7

A man sat in an up-scale restaurant behind a table dressed in linen and the finest tableware. He ordered an exceptional wine from an extensive list and a la carte from a carefully crafted menu. The kitchen was staffed by a world reknown chef and his team. When the wine came the man criticized its bouquet. When the food came he nit-picked each course, all the while fussing about the service.

A woman returned from visiting her missionary brother who served in a poverty-stricken country. When asked about the people there one of her comments was, "They praise God joyfully for things I could never eat."

Among the casualties of our materialistic culture are joy and gratitude. These are predictable consequences when we devote ourselves to the preening of our appetites. Our expectations run away with themselves. Look around you. Even if you live with modest means, chances are your home is filled with more than you need. Under such circumstances you would think that your joy and gratitude would be epidemic, contagious. Are they?

I knew a man once who had reached great heights on the corporate ladder. According to the common wisdom he "had it all." Over time, he lost his edge in business then his job. He was forced to downsize. His wife, who had become accustomed to the perks of affluence, left him, taking everything she could in the divorce. Eventually he found his way to the church door. He was living in a small apartment and working in a job well under his qualifications. As we sat having coffee after worship one Sunday he expressed gratitude for his new life. "I never thought I'd be saying this," he told me, "but in a way I'm actually glad everything fell apart. I see the little things now and I'm thankful for every day."

Feeding the unrequited appetites of the self and living with a profound sense of gratitude tend to be mutually exclusive. There is nothing complicated about this. If you sow unto yourself and your wants, you will reap the weeds of ingratitude and insatiable desire. If you invest the day with the currency of gratitude, even the smallest thing can provide the occasion to "praise God joyfully."

**"All this is from God, who through Christ reconciled us to Himself."
2 Corinthians 5:18**

Paul writes here of reconciliation, a new relationship bringing together God and humanity in Jesus Christ. We do not earn this reconciliation. The will cannot will it. We do not prove we are worthy of it nor can we keep it by our own strength. This new relationship with God is built upon a foundation far more enduring than anything we can offer.

Being reconciled, we are not only summoned to be different people. That is not good enough. We are killed and made alive. We are recreated. We are new creatures. God has brought something new which is at work in us to conquer the powers of sin, death and evil. The center of this wonderful, reconciling miracle is God Himself, crucified and risen.

In Baptism God claims us, adopts us, makes us His own. The reconciliation is God's gift, given out of His great love. We are saved by His grace through faith. In Christ, God came to us, died for us, was raised for us. He gives us the Holy Spirit, drawing us to Himself through Word and Sacrament. He clears away the debris of our past, continually opening for us a reconciled future. One day, He will complete the work of salvation and usher us into the eternal kingdom.

"All this is from God," for which we are duty bound to "thank, praise, serve and obey Him."

"Now Jesus did many other signs in the presence of the disciples, which are not written in this book; but these are written that you may believe that Jesus is the Christ, the Son of God, and that believing you may have life in his name." John 20:30-31

You can find any number of books, sermons, etc, that point to the healing/miracle stories in the Gospels as illustrations of the compassion of Jesus and how we should be compassionate also. No doubt that element is there, but it is not primary. The miracles of Jesus were not ends in themselves. They were signs, arrows pointing to Jesus. Some got it and some did not.

The Gospel of John, for example, tells of the raising of Lazarus from the dead. One can definitely not conclude that because Jesus raised the dead, we should hang around in graveyards praying for the ground to open up. Don ot try this at home! Jesus raised Lazarus as a sign to bring the focus on Himself. "I am the resurrection and life," He said," The words and works of Jesus, taken together, are a tapestry that spells out His name. The signs are given that you "may believe" in Jesus.

John's Gospel likes the phrase "believe in" where Jesus is concerned. That is different than believing Jesus. I may believe what you say, but that sort of belief implies no necessary relationship or commitment of trust or faith. It may mean nothing more than intellectual assent. If I believe *in* the one who speaks, that is different.

The identity of Jesus was never obvious. That has not changed. The Church at times may speak as if His identity as "true God and true man" should be obvious, but this is nothing more than triumphalism.

The outcome of trust, of faith, is life; "...that you may have life in His name", is the way John states it. John is saying if you don't have Jesus, you are dead. You may be walking and talking, putting a day together and so forth, but that is not life the faith is talking about.

Among the four great witnesses to Jesus - Matthew, Mark, Luke and John, none speak with more clarity, simplicity and urgency than John. And the urgency with which he writes points us to Jesus and to the fact that trusting, that believing *in* him is a matter, in every sense, of death and life.

"For since in the wisdom of God the world through its wisdom did not come to know God, God was well-pleased through the foolishness of the message preached to save those who believe."
1 Corinthians 1:21

"Actions speak louder than words". So the saying goes. Or, "Sticks and stones may break my bones but words can never harm me." Someone once said, "Your actions are speaking so loudly I can't hear what you are saying." If we say things like this often enough and loud enough the impression is left that words are not that important.

The Church is also caught up in the problem. We hear the same kinds of comments within Church life. A personal experience with God is more important than doctrine. Faith means one does not need to understand, just believe. But believe what? Faith accepts certain things are mysteries. But what mysteries? Somehow or another we thrive on anti-verbal religion.

Faith, belief and mystery do not mean muddle. They do not imply that the Christian can say anything where God is concerned. For faith, words are attached, for us, to what has been revealed and made known about God in the Bible.

At the same time words are fuzzy - all words. We may prefer those who "say what they mean and mean what they say" but that is just an expression. Communication is not that simple. The basic problem, therefore, is that our words are both important and fuzzy.

Finally, it is important to note that words are actions. Try yelling "Fire!" in a crowded room and you'll find out quickly that words have real effect. Martin Luther was so convinced that words equal action that he called the church a "mouth house." For it is through the Church's words that the Holy Spirit "calls, gathers, enlightens sanctifies" us in faith. Saint Paul put it this way: "Faith comes by hearing..." and what is heard is the message of Christ.

It may seem odd to us that God would choose words to be the vehicle which brings the new creation, but should it? After all, the old creation, as Genesis tells us, was spoken into existence. If God could use a word to bring something out of nothing, then He can certainly use the spoken word of His law and His Gospel to bring the new creation in Jesus Christ upon you.

It's Personal

Rocker Mick Jagger – who is not your garden variety theologian - had a song lyric years ago which went something like, "Don't want to hear any more about Jesus, I just want to see His face."That reflects what an awful lot of people would want to say: enough talk, enough theology, we just want to see Jesus. And of course, we find this in the new testament. A man came to the disciples and said, "Sir, we would see Jesus." So, it's a personal thing.

We can look at the Bible, and if we pick it up with that handle, we can see that the Biblical story is a series of personal relationships, encounters with God.

God goes to Noah and says it may be dry now, but rain is coming, lots of it, and you need to build a very large boat. Noah's not so sure but he builds it anyway. He wouldn't do that unless there was something very personal going on between God and himself.

God comes to Abraham and says, "Abe, I want you to pack up and leave this place. Oh and by the way I'm not going to tell you where you are going, Maybe later. Just go." Well that is not the kind of thing one does on the basis of test tubes and calculators. Abraham did that because he was overwhelmed by this very personal word from God.

God speaks to the prophets. And this also seems to be intensely personal because they seem to be the only ones that know what the message is. And the word of the Lord came to Jeremiah. The word of the Lord came to Isaiah, etc.

Jesus comes to Matthew in the toll gate, singles him out and talks to him. Zacchaeus up in the tree is called down by Jesus and they go to lunch.

The Samaritan woman at the well – Jesus asks for a drink of water then begins to speak of the intimate details of her life.

At the end of the day, there can be no substitute for this personal dimension. "For God so loved the world..."means God loves you and me. Theological reflection on the faith is necessary. But if it does not lead to the proclamation of the Word of the Gospel as an apocalyptic, personal, gracious encounter with God, it has missed its point – and redemptive purpose.

"So the law is our tutor to bring us to Christ, that we might be justified by faith. But now faith that is come, we are no longer under a tutor. For you are all sons of God, through faith, in Christ Jesus. For as many of you as were baptized into Christ have put on Christ." Galatians 3:24

From the moment of our Baptism God has held us in the spontaneous life of the Spirit. As sons and daughters we have been called to live freely in the Spirit, not by the letter of the law but by grace. The Christian faith has always struggled with this freedom. The New Testament itself grapples with it. Paul embraces this freedom with a frightening certainty. James seems to be hedging his bets. Has God given us in this freedom a load that is too much for us to bear? Is the water too deep? That depends.

As the freedom of the Gospel coaxes the Christian into deeper water the old sinner in us, standing comfortably in the shallows and equipped with the security of the law, immediately mounts a defense: "You just can't do what you want! God wants obedience after all! Stay safely within the Law."

If freedom only serves to evoke this self conscious awareness of my lack of freedom, I will be tempted to turn to the Law for remediation, balance and security. And when I do, I may discover a kind of relief being moored to the Law. I will find a kind of comfortable certainty there that freedom simply does not give. When the Christian lives this way, daring only to wade into the shallows of freedom, a little bit of freedom is all you get. The Church has stood in the shallows of freedom for much of its history.

If my freedom, however, is informed not by fear and self-consciousness but by the Cross, something else happens. I am taken out of myself and taken up into the spontaneous life of Christ, the life of the Spirit. When the Cross is the starting and ending point of faith, Christ becomes the end of the law. I am able to plunge headlong into the deep waters of faith, hope and love, into the depths of the grace that has set me free.

"In Christ all things cohere." Colossians 1:17

Millions of people today live their lives in fragments. One experience or one moment is episodic, detached from a greater whole. The result of this meandering is a culture where neurosis is epidemic. Drugs, alcohol and a thousand other diversions are used to mask the sense of life's ultimate meaninglessness. What does the Christian faith have to say to these who in one way or another are debilitated by this crisis of hopelessness?

When Jesus spoke of the integrating power of God, He spoke of the Kingdom of God, which is better translated, The 'Rule' or 'Reign' of God'. ' "The Kingdom of God has come near you," He proclaimed. In Jesus Christ God has addressed the cognitive dissonance of meaning by reaffirming His gracious and determined commitment to the world. Years later, as Paul reflected on the faith, he came to see the Cross, the Crucified Christ as that great, integrating moment when all the fragments of this life were gathered up in God's all-embracing mercy and grace.

If the Church is going to be a faithful witness to the Gospel in this time, we cannot afford to meet this crisis with indifference. We dare not close the blinds. What God has united on the Cross we have no right to separate. Which is to say, since Christ has died for all, all people are our concern. The mandate is simple. We are called to proclaim the reconciliation that is in Jesus and with some joy, too.

So whether in dialogue with the lost wanderer or the self-satisfied secularist, our goal is the same: to bear witness in all humanity and humility to that power of God, unleashed in the Gospel of Jesus the crucified One, that the world might believe, and in believing find reconciliation, coherence and purpose in Him.

The Cultural Air

Several years ago, Linda and I were in Venice, Italy on a Sunday morning and decided to attend worship in one of the local churches, Santa Maria della Salute. The building is a large, beautiful structure, erected long ago in thanks for relief from a plague. And it was nearly empty.

What had happened that could create such a disconnect between the people who raised this building at enormous cost and great effort, and the people of today?

The hypothesis of God is simply not needed by millions of people today in order to inhabit the institutions and roles of society. Take a deep breath of the cultural air, in Venice, Italy or in Orange County, California, and this is what you get:

First, life is the product of blind forces and blind chance. Natural forces are without mind and without purpose. Everything is accidental.

Second, you only go around once. Death is the ultimate tragedy so deny it as much as possible.

Third, the language of absolutes is to be avoided. We must speak in the terms of relativism, opinions, climates, attitudes, feelings. No one is right. Religion is privatized. In such a climate we are really quite unhappy with anything but pragmatic and temporary solutions. No one size fits all, please.

Fourth, you and I are on our own in the world. We make our own meaning. I will do it on my own if I can, in community with others if I must, but meaning is self-created.

With this cultural oxygen passing through our lungs, churches are perceived by many as peripheral and irrelevant. For them, God-language speaks about a cult deity around whom a few people gather but not a God that necessarily must lead to the use of religious language that speaks meaningfully to all aspects of daily life. It is not hard to see how these cultural axioms conflict profoundly with the Sunday morning confession, "I believe in God the Father, Creator of heaven and earth." For six and one half days a week we are pressured to compartmentalize this belief in a Creator and then, only on Sunday, confess one.

Johnny One Note

A small town parade was making its way down Main Street. Floats provided by various community groups sailed slowly along as the high school marching band stepped lively, accompanying itself with a rousing march. But the center o attention, literally, was none of this. For as the parade moved along, the folks gathered on the sidewalks applauded wildly for the six year old boy who, equipped with a toy trumpet, had inserted himself into the parade. Resolute and determined he kept his own pace, all the while sounding one, solitary note on his little trumpet.

The purpose of Christian proclamation is to bear witness to Jesus Christ, especially His Cross. The Resurrection must also be taken with radical seriousness, but not at the expense of the Cross. For, beginning with Saint Paul, the exalted Lord is proclaimed as the One who was crucified. But why? Why this one, solitary note where Jesus is concerned?

The Cross surely does say to us that God is there in the deepest valleys and hurts of life, even unto death. But first and foremost, the Cross proclaims that God meets us precisely at the point of our deepest need, the very point where we reject Him, on the Cross itself. This is why the central Gospel word, spoken from the Cross, is the Word of forgiveness. Forgiveness, reconciliation with God is our deepest need.

The Cross is also the Church's solitary note because we proclaim a hidden God, not a God breaking out in all kinds of glory, not in this life. God's glory parades around in weakness and lowliness. God the Word comes in simple words, water, bread and wine. The driving purpose of this hidden God is to bury Himself so deeply within the muck and mire of our sin that we simply give up, die and glory in nothing except the Cross of our Lord Jesus, "...through which the world has been crucified to me and I to the world."

So, the next time you're in some church, whatever else they are parading around, hope and pray that you hear little "Johnny One Note" playing the scandalous, solitary Word of the Cross. For in that one note of the Cross is contained the fullness of God's grand symphony of love and grace - and it sounds for you.

Abandon the battlefield?

I once spoke with a war veteran who had been involved in the most intense combat. He recalled a day when the fighting was so fierce and the bombardment so unrelenting that he was tempted to preserve himself and desert the battlefield. It was only the discipline of his training and loyalty to his fellow soldiers that made it possible for him to hold his position.

There is a kind of metaphor for living in this episode. Life is full of temptations to "abandon the battlefield." This has always been so but I cannot help but wonder if this is not a particular feature of our time.

The Christian dare not abandon life, for to do so is tantamount to proclaiming that God has abandoned the world. Some simple disciplines can help.

First, along with exposure to the news, control your input by reading your Bible daily. Beginning and ending your day with the Scriptures serves as a continuing reminder that God is always around. You can start and end the day by being reminded of the latest outrage or God's great promises.

Second, say your prayers. Even if your prayers are complaints, throw them to heaven. God hears even when no one else does. You are not in this fight alone.

Third, join others in worship. Worship is the gathering of your comrades in arms, where through the Word and sacraments we are equipped for spiritual warfare, given strength and assurance for the horizontal dimension of hope as we live in and engage the world for the kingdom. Worship is also a living metaphor that tips hope on its vertical axis, reminding us that we are a forever-people, captured and held by the grace of our crucified and Risen Lord, destined for eternity. Worship lifts our eyes toward the larger vision.

Regular Bible reading, prayer and worship give the life of faith coherence, vision, joy, and that courage in Christ which resists the temptation to "abandon the battlefield" of living.

"For I decided to know nothing among you except Jesus Christ and him crucified." 1 Corinthians 2:2

Johann Sebastian Bach is known for his mastery of the 'fugue,' a musical form built around one, recurring theme. Bach's 'Art of the Fugue' is a collection of brilliantly constructed fugues that exemplify the form. So much so that they can be played by virtually any instrumental combination with satisfying effect.

Bach offers an insight into the nature and purpose of theology, of the Christian witness. Like the winding counterpoint of the fugue, the great theme of the Cross may be amplified in any number of voices. Indeed, it should be. But if that theme is broken or lost, the composition wanders aimlessly. The composition is disharmonious and ultimately pointless.

One can sense today the widespread confusion regarding the Christian faith. There are many voices, but the counterpoint often lacks harmony and focus. When the message of the Cross falls out of the center of the Christian witness, disharmony results. Saint Paul was among the first Christians that we know of to tap the podium in an effort to get the attention of the members of the orchestra who were wandering off into themes of their own making. He heard, as we can today, elements of the Church that were losing their voice for the Cross.

This is not to say that the Cross is not widely talked about today. But much of that talk "spins" the Cross to be a moment of divine identification with us poor victims of whatever injustice we feel has come upon us. Poor Jesus was a victim, too. So He can relate. He can identify with us and we with Him. But this is not the message of the Cross. This is not the theme

What, then, is the great fugal theme of the faith? On the Cross God seals the exits so that there is only one way out. That way is the crucified and Risen Lord Himself. The Cross does not identify with us. It indicts us. At the same time, the great theme of the Cross rings with the sound of pure grace. "Father, forgive them," he said. If the Cross indicts us in our godlessness, even more does it reveal God precisely where He means to be found, in the suffering and dying Jesus where God moves against us and, in sheer mercy, for us.

174

"Do your best to present yourself to God as one approved, a workman who has no need to be ashamed, rightly handling the word of truth." 2 Timothy 2:15

There is a book in my library which deals with classical art. But the period of classical art does not exist except in someone's mind. Classical art is a category that is imposed on historical persons, sculptures, paintings, architecture and so forth. Classical art is a category because enough people have studied certain similarities and groupings have agreed upon the term. So, art and architectural historians generalize using the term 'classical'.

It is absurd to say we cannot generalize. We have to generalize and categorize. It is absolutely essential to human life.

The real issue is not that we categorize or generalize. The question is whether we do it well or badly. This brings me to the subject of Christian doctrine.

There is a widespread impatience and weariness today (notice, I am generalizing) with respect to doctrine. I have heard television preachers, for example, say with pride to large masses of approving listeners that they do not preach doctrine. They only preach the Bible. At which point they launch into sermons that are laced with doctrinal statements. This is dishonest, of course. This is simply an example of handling doctrine badly, of not "rightly handling the word of truth."

There are three components of faith: knowledge, assent and trust. All three are important but must be handled with some care or we end up in the ditch. One ditch is to say that faith is only knowledge and assent.

Another ditch is to say that you just have faith. Down with doctrine! But faith in what? The Great Pumpkin? The Tooth Fairy? To claim faith without knowledge or assent is to begin faith within yourself.

As the Church reflects upon the God of the Bible it categorizes the Bible's witness into generalized statements regarding God the Father, Jesus, the Holy Spirit, sin, creation and numerous other aspects of the faith. Christians do not always agree on these generalizations but they are important, necessary and essential.

175

"He descended into hell."

Preaching on hell in the post-modern world is a bit like telling scary stories to frighten children. It is hardly the proper subject for the mature and enlightened. Millions of people, both within the Church as well as without, will hear no talk of hell for they are quite certain it does not exist.

In the early 1980's a group of us toured what was then East Germany. It was the 450th anniversary of Martin Luther's birth. One of our stops was the concentration camp at Buchenwald. As we walked over the ground which had been the scene of premeditated mass murder one of our group said, "It must have been hell." It was the right choice of words. Nothing else would do. The words written over Dante's gate to hell could have been written over the gate to Buchenwald, "Abandon hope all you who enter here."

Our experience of being together may teach us that even as we attempt to create our versions of heaven on earth we also create our versions of hell on earth. We may not hear this in the churches anymore but television, movies, novels and plays scream these themes at us day and night. We desire friendliness and recognition but all too often we receive - and give - contempt and suffering. We turn each other's lives into a living hell on such a scale the sheer ordinariness of it is staggering.

Jesus came proclaiming and living among us the nearness of God's kingdom. Yet we made His life unbearable, finally giving Him a taste of hell on the Cross. One more victim of the death dealers. What made Jesus' death unique, however, is that this one who experienced profound abandonment ("My God, my God, why have you forsaken me?"), is the same one who lived in the full consciousness of God's presence ("The Father and I are one").

This is why Christians have taken such comfort in the knowledge that the just and righteous one was abandoned to hell's fury. For if the Son of God, in whom God and life in their fullness dwelled, was subject to death and hell, then we may no longer look to ourselves to break the impasse of evil. Instead, we are summoned, as Luther proclaimed, to "Look to the wounds of Christ, for there has your hell been mastered."

The Church

In my Lutheran tradition the definition of Church can be found in our confessional documents: "The Church is where the Word is rightly preached and the Sacraments properly administered." But where exactly is this happening? What is the Gospel, anyway? And how many church-going people would be able to tell if their own pastors are preaching it rightly, let alone those in other churches? Furthermore there are Lutheran hurch bodies that have little do with one another and even now Lutherans are splitting into groups, once again, over differences. And that is just one tradition among many that are embroiled in nasty church fights.

In one sense to say "The Lutherans believe..." or "The Catholics believe..." or "The Baptists believe..." is practically meaningless. Some have taken to using the term "non-denominational" in an effort to sidestep all this denominational division. But they, too, have varying points of view, so their term is misleading and contributes nothing. In every case I cannot help but hear the admonition of Saint Paul to the Corinthians, writing of the Church, the body of Christ:

"The eye cannot say to the hand, 'I don't need you!' And the head cannot say to the feet, 'I don't need you!'
Really, Paul? It appears to me that 'I don't need you' is among the most well-rehearsed phrases in all corners of the Church.

This is not the place to address the many questions such observations raise. But a clear-headed view of they way things actually are should, at the very least, open our eyes to the fact that millions of people look at the Church and find our witness trivial and unconvincing. This should call forth some measure of humility among those of us who so glibly toss the word Church around like we hold exclusive title to it.

As we Christians stumble along in our pride and confusion, the Creed reminds us that this side of heaven the Church will always be an article of faith, resisting our sight. Therefore, as I survey the mess that is the Church, and of which I am a part, it is readily apparent, at least to me, that the best I can do is dare to trust that it is this feeble, struggling communion of saints that God in His grace has chosen and through which He offers Himself for the sake of the world.

"Because I live." John 14:19

The entire witness of the New Testament is predicated upon the events of the cross and resurrection. There is not one line in any of the twenty seven books that even remotely attempts to memorialize a dead Jesus. On the contrary. Every line assumes the event of the Resurrection. As difficult as it may be for reason to come to terms with this, faith can speak of the bodily Resurrection of Jesus only as an act of God

The brutal suffering and death of Jesus left the disciples in despair. They were a broken, defeated remnant of a lost cause. What revived them? Did they simply "look on the bright side" and give themselves a pep talk and say things like' 'Let's carry on for good ol' Jesus'? On the contrary, their faith was not revived by anything they did. The most obvious explanation for their transformation is the one given by the New Testament witness; the one whom they saw crucified, dead and buried, they also saw alive and arisen from the grave.

With the appearance of the Risen Lord the disciples were brought face to face with the fact that while Jesus lived, they were the ones who had succumbed to death. Their despair, faithlessness and refusal to believe what he had told them of His death and resurrection simply confirmed their deadness. If Jesus was the dead One who was now living, the disciples were the living dead.

And is this not our position in a blind, fallen world? We wring our hands in despair and anxiety over our lost innocence, broken dreams and the myriad injustices all around us. We stand before the seductions, enchantments, terrors and threats of the world and allow them, rather than "Every Word that proceeds from the mouth of God", to shape and define our hearts. But this glaring contrast was not the end of the story for the disciples and it is not the end for us. For Jesus, alive and risen from the dead, called them to life! "Because I live", he promised, "so will you."

God's Peace and Justice

According to some current standard accounts of the Christian faith, the Christian message is a call to social and economic justice, radical inclusiveness and unconditional affirmation. Is this the best the Church can do?

Let us be clear. Working for social and economic justice are fine, even necessary ends as we carry out our human duties and responsibilities. But there is nothing uniquely Christian about being concerned with these things. Jesus did not have to die on the Cross in order for us to see the self-interest inherent in these matters of justice. These are issues that occupy the concern of the entire human race. No religious sensibility, Christian or otherwise, is necessary to have these concerns.

Christians also have a stake in working for a just world insofar as they are possible. But that is just the point. In a sinful world, estranged from God, they are finally not possible. If you take the Bible seriously, or even if you do not, read the first three chapters of the Book of Romans and then see if you have any illusions left about our capacity to bring about a peaceful and just world.

The Christian cause cannot finally be equated with propping up the human project no matter how noble the effort. Saint Paul, no stranger to encouraging Christians to care for others, understood this very well. He sets the Church straight when he admonishes that the first and primary business of the Church is to proclaim the crucified and risen Christ (to know nothing except Christ crucified.) For it is in the foolishness of what we preach (Paul's words) that God rescues sinners from sin, death and the power of evil, by the peace and justice offered through Christ's death on the Cross and His Resurrection.

The Church is distinguished primarily by its message, not its works. Therefore, the work that should occupy the center of the church's life is the life-line of the Gospel's proclamation, which announces the peace of God that comes through a living relationship with Jesus Christ, and the justice of God through which sinners are declared righteous, forgiven and free, by grace through faith, for Jesus sake!

"Put the X back in Xmas."

One year in December a bookstore displayed a large banner across the front window that read: "Put the X back in Xmas." I am pretty certain it was meant to be cynical, but in an odd way it said something important. Put the "X" back in Christmas. Put the "Cross" back in Christmas. The birth of Jesus by itself never saved anyone. Shocking, but true. We may miss the heart of the Gospel—the Son's obedience even unto death—if we do not include it also at Christmas, the one Christian festival the world most embraces.

At Christmas we tend to pause and rest and even settle in to marvel at the birth of Jesus – and that is good. For in the end, the nativity of Christ is not a problem to be solved, it is a mystery to be celebrated and wondered at. At the same time, a caution is in order. The widespread popularity – and I use that word purposely – can be largely attributed to the aggressive marketing it receives from the mercantile culture. As some one once remarked, if Christmas didn't exist our capitalist system would have had to invent something like it.

For the earliest Christians, however, the birth of Christ was never the main point. When Jesus began his ministry, most people had no idea when or where he was born. His birth was not widely observed by the early Christians for several centuries and even then was celebrated only to oppose a pagan festival. The few Gospel references to his birth link it to rejection and violence: for example, Herod seeks to use the wise men to find Jesus so that he can kill him. When that fails, Herod kills all the male infants in the vicinity of Bethlehem in a futile attempt to be rid of this newborn king. The songs of Mary and Simeon mention the conflict that Jesus' coming will bring.

The alarming scandal of the entire Jesus story is in its concreteness, its simple worldliness, in its claim that God will not be found in philosophical speculations or in the currently fashionable doctrine of religious equivalency but where He means to be found – in the babe of Bethlehem, in the crucified and risen One, accessible now in Word and sacrament.

Pride

Martin Luther once said, "The law is for the proud." He knew what he was talking about. And the prayer of the proud is that of the man in the New Testament: "I thank you, God, that I am not like other men."

The Greek word which we translate to mean 'pride' can also mean haughtiness and arrogance. The prideful believe that by denigrating others they elevate themselves.

So you can see how the word is an apt description of many who invest their lives in material wealth or attempt to live according to religious principles. The proud are so self-obsessed they simply do not see things as they are. This is the awareness that lies behind the Lord's words in the text from John 9. To be spiritually blinded by pride is to be out of touch with reality, no matter how knowledgeable or intelligent we may be. And His words are as timely as ever, for we live in an age infected by pride and its toxic consequences.

In the same comment Martin Luther also said, "The Gospel is for the brokenhearted." As the religiously proud man stood on that ancient street corner, exalting himself to the heavens, a despised tax collector was also praying nearby. The man was so in touch with himself before God he could not bring himself to even look toward heaven. He prayed to this effect, "God be merciful to me a sinner." After Jesus told this story He said,

"I tell you that this man, rather than the other, went home justified before God. For everyone who exalts himself will be humbled, and he who humbles himself will be exalted."

The proud, and we ALL find ourselves owning the word in one way or another, refuse humility and in so doing subvert life and distort its purpose. But God is not mocked. The artificial life produced by pride will always collapse into meaninglessness.

It is of the essence of the Incarnation that Jesus humbled Himself. His very life was a judgment upon our pride and willfulness; pride and willfulness he endured even to death on the Cross. When we see ourselves in this light, it just might bring us to sobriety and enable us to utter those words which are the key to freedom and authentic life, "God, be merciful to me, a sinner."

"Do not judge, or you too will be judged...first take the plank out of your own eye, and then you will see clearly to remove the speck from your brother's eye." Matthew 7:1

With the benefit of age, I can see far more clearly the carefree days of youth, when I was confident that the future was now and all that mattered was the present. Decades of living have tempered this rashness until now there is a sobriety and humility about life.

The assertions that drove me to self-hood and independence also turned out to be a willfulness that took me beyond the restrictions and standards meant to keep me safe, into places I should have avoided, and steered my life in ways both great and small onto the shoals of grief and heartache. I discovered that in a thousand ways the downward pull of the world was more than a match. It was then that life became a juggling act of living with the contaminations of compromise and the tempering of disappointment .

A lot can be said about this but I want to make a singular point. Decades in the pastoral ministry have shown me that far too many people in the church seem to have no capacity to recognize this struggle in the lives of others, nor do they honestly confront it in themselves. The Church seems too often to be a place where it is permissible to come down on the defections of others, thanking God we are not like them, as if we are not bound in our own willfulness and pretensions.

Christian people are to take their cues from the one who went to the Cross, the one who said, "Do not judge, or you too will be judged...first take the plank out of your own eye, and then you will see clearly to remove the speck from your brother's eye."

The convoluted shamble of your life, however well you may be hiding it, has only one antidote: the contagion of God's love and mercy in Jesus. And for this anecdote you can offer nothing. It is God's free and gracious gift to you. It is this mercy that restores us, not to idealism but to hope. For that hope cannot be compared to the frantic idealisms of the world. It is rooted in God's promises, and it will never disappoint.

"For me, to live is Christ..." Philippians 1:21

The late Dr. George Forell, in his book The Proclamation of the Gospel in a Pluralistic World, outlines three levels of religious commitment. With regard to the Bible, for example, those on the first level say it is an important book but it is rarely if ever read.

A second-level view is that it is a good book. When it is read, it is often to search out axioms or moral principles for living.

A minority share the third level view: the Bible is the inspired Word of God, through which the Holy Spirit works to create a living faith in Christ. They read the Scriptures regularly and gather with others to hear the Word of God proclaimed.

Another area which Dr. Forell describes is the Church. On one level a person says, "I was raised a Lutheran." "Going to church" is a matter of pedigree, a religious necessity.

On the second level, the majority, say the Church is where we learn about right and wrong. For them, "going to church" is a gathering of the morally concerned. The Church is a vehicle to attempt a moral life.

The third level, a minority, sees the Church as a body of believers, the people of God, summoned through the Gospel to bring the world to the Cross, that there they might know their Savior. They do not "go to church", they are the Church: the gathering of the forgiven who have been "called and sanctified" in faith through Jesus Christ.

It is to this third level that our Lord Jesus called the Twelve and to which He calls you and me through Word and sacrament. Followers, disciples, believers, whatever words we use, are ordinary people made extraordinary by the love and grace of God. These people do not "go to church" as if it was simply one more event on the weekly calendar. For them, as Saint Paul has written, "to live is Christ." By lives devoted to thanksgiving, praise and love of others, they seek to show what and Who they believe is really worth living for.

"Not by bread alone." Matthew 4:4

Even many of the poor today live in far better conditions than most of the people who have ever lived. So, given the material and other comforts humans enjoy in our country and elsewhere on this tiny orb, why is not the world brimming over with happiness?

The truth is that while we need a certain level of provision and comfort to live, a satisfied life is not finally a result of these things. This should be obvious to us by now, but we continue to make cliches of ourselves and look to those things that cannot satisfy. How many dreary stories have we heard of those who fill their bank accounts, or try to, only to discover, in a thousand ways, that full banks often reflect an empty life.

For all our complexities, certain things about human beings are quite straightforward. Our Lord Jesus had a way of putting a laser beam on this fact with words like this:

"Man does not live by bread alone, but by every word that proceeds from the mouth of God."

This is a statement of fact that cuts right to the bone. After all, how many of us in actual fact, do believe and live as if "bread alone" in all its forms is actually enough?

A full, abundant, satisfied - that is to say, authentically human life - was never meant to result from grabbing at the material. Another laser beam from the Lord put it this way:

"What does it profit a man if he should gain the whole world and lose his soul?" In our daily pursuit of "gold and goods" these words of Christ Jesus are not simply a gentle reminder, a mild piece of advice. They are words of promise, a two-edged sword that cuts two ways.

Promise One: Seek your life through the material alone and an authentic life of love, joy and peace will elude you. Promise Two: Seek your life under the promises of God's Word in Christ Jesus and the love, joy, peace - and contentment - that are in Him will bring your anxious heart to rest. For when you have Him, you have everything. The rest is icing on the cake!

"But the very hairs of your head are all numbered." Matthew 10:30

Among the more obvious contemporary examples of unrestrained cynicism is the slogan adopted by those who are marketing Las Vegas to the masses, 'What Happens in Vegas, Stays in Vegas." When I was a rock musician back in the sixties the same concept had a slightly different slant, "What Happens on Tour, Stays On Tour."

The lure in this enticing fiction is that it is possible to engage in human behavior that avoids scrutiny and accountability and is beyond judgment. Why anyone who has any regard for others would want to actively promote this idea and encourage others to do so is hard to fathom.

The slogan also has the dead ring of nihilism about it. Can what I do be brought before no higher court than myself? Is life devoid of any higher significance?

Jesus pointed out to those around Him that God's eye perceives the tiny sparrow and as well as every hair on your head. These words can have the effect of bringing great comfort but they also just might bring something else. It makes a difference if one is conscious that all of life, from the inside out, lies under the unblinking eye of the Creator. Nothing escapes scrutiny, no thought, word or deed escapes notice.

The early Christians were encouraged to "walk as children of the light." It is a good phrase and an even better way of life. Children of the light are out in the open. Their 'yes' is yes and their 'no' is no. At the first sign of dawn they do not close the blinds or scurry under rocks. But who among us would dare on our own claim such a title? How dare we who have walked in darkness, and for whom innocence is no longer a possibility, claim the title "Children of the Light?"

We may dare such a life because the Great Eye of God has looked upon us in forgiving love in Jesus Christ, not holding the "deeds of darkness" against us. "While we were yet sinners, Christ died for us," the Word proclaims. Now, in the light of His amazing grace, we may live out in the open freely, knowing that when God's complete knowledge of us becomes too much, and drives us into the darkness, it is only so that we may return to the welcoming arms of God's forgiveness.

The Myth of free Will

Ask most Americans what they value most and the response will probably be 'freedom'. Ask them to define freedom and the answers will have something to do with being able to do as we please. Interestingly, the founders of this country defined freedom as being able to do as we ought, not necessarily as we please.

Freedom is actually defined by its choices as reflected in this classic definition:

"Freedom is the absence of necessity, coercion or constraint in choice or action."

The implications are obvious. Authentic freedom only belongs to those who always and in every thought, word and deed choose the right and the good. A simple inventory of our own life's timeline of thoughts, words and deeds, will reveal that we are anything but free. For our choices of thoughts, words and deeds often reflect not the absence but the presence of "necessity, coercion, or constraint in choice or action." And that which is present in us driving these things is sin.

We don't like hearing this of course. 'What do you mean I'm not free? Of course I am! I have free will, don't I?" Actually, there is a no better witness against us than our so-called free will. It is our ample backlog of free willed thoughts, words and deeds that contain the record of the countless ways we have chosen the bad instead of the good. This is the truth. And unless we know and hear the truth about ourselves, we will continue to live the lie, calling bondage freedom. But the implications are even more serious.

True freedom belongs to God alone. Only God is free, because only God's willing always, and in every sense results in the good. This is why to claim freedom for yourself - including free will - is, in fact, blasphemy against God. For such a claim shows contempt for God , wittingly or not, by claiming for yourself something that belongs to God alone.

Jesus said, "He who sins is a slave to sin." You are not free. And because of sin we have no permanent place with God. For the wages of sin is death. But to this sobering reality our Lord added an even greater truth: "If the Son sets you free, you will be free indeed."

Good Hymns

My late friend, Pastor Herb Brokering, once told the story of the Mudderhouse he visited in former East Germany. The Mudderhouse was a medical clinic staffed by Christian people who cared for the sick in that place. Every morning, the nurses went into each room and sang hymns to the patients. They sang the traditional hymns of the Church and the themes they carried into the lives of the sick and dying were those of the grace, love, mercy, hope, and forgiveness that is in Jesus Christ.

Hymns are really nothing more than praise, petitions, and proclamation set to music. And the subject of all hymns is, finally, God. I am always on guard for hymns where the language of the texts dwell on 'we' and 'I'. A careful study of many contemporary hymn texts will reveal a heavy emphasis on these words used in an overly-emotional way. Those words may be appropriate, of course, but an over-emphasis on them can twist a hymn all out of shape.

A good hymn takes us out of ourselves and provides a vehicle that directs our prayer and praise toward the God who comes to us in mercy and love. A good hymn puts words in our mouths which permit us to sing the tune of the self in a diminutive minor key, while singing of God and His glory in Jesus Christ with all the stops pulled out.

Two Freedoms

When that little bundle of unrealized wonderfulness called Mark Anderson came home from the hospital, my parents soon realized that I was also a bundle of something not quite so wonderful - stubborn willfulness, intent on having it my way. The game was on! This is why, along with all its joys, parenthood also placed on my folks the roles of accuser, arresting officer, prosecutor, judge and jailer. It is only as I grew, and learned to live under the obligations of family life, that I was released into the wider world and ever-expanding obligations.

The continuing refinement of obligation which begins with parenting and extends into the wider society through law is a process which attempts to check the abuse of a flawed freedom. The endless proliferation of laws in every country, for example, is a symptom of this abuse.

When Saint Paul tells us that "Christ has set us free," what sort of freedom is he speaking of? It surely cannot mean temporal freedom to do as we will, to simply have the ability to choose among options. Neither does it mean disengagement from life, having leisure time, independent wealth or being on vacation.

The freedom of the Christian is two things at once. On the one hand, Christian freedom is the gift of complete and total identification with Jesus Christ. All the benefits of Christ are given to the Christian. Nothing is held back. This is why Jesus could say, "When the Son makes you free, you are free indeed."

At the same time Christian freedom is total engagement in life. And it must be. For there can be no hiding behind prefabricated solutions for the freedom of faith. And this is what we recoil from. This is what we fear. The freedom God grants is so complete that we are thrust onto the stage of life as "lambs of among wolves," seemingly unprepared for so great a freedom in a world so bound in its pretensions and law.

The ringing note of this glorious freedom so struck the Apostle Paul that he could sum up the whole Christian life in one, simple declaration, "For freedom Christ has set us free."

"But God showed His love for us that while we were yet sinners Christ died for us." Romans 5:8

I sat with a couple who were preparing for marriage. The young woman ran through a lengthy list of all the reasons she could think of as to why she loved her fiance. He was generous, hard-working, handsome, thoughtful, funny, and so forth. When it was time for the young man to speak he said," I don't need a reason to love her. I just love her. I want her happiness more than I do my own." He was not far from the Kingdom!

When we examine the Bible it does not provide us with God's reasons for loving. Nowhere is there an assessment of humanity from God's vantage point where He lists our numerous virtues as reason for loving us. If anything, the Bible is a collection of evidence that suggests there is not much lovable about us. Our generous self-assessments are not reflected in the mirror of heaven. This is hard for us to take, to be sure. There must be something in me that God values, something I can do or be, some potential, at least, that God sees in me.

If that is so, then God's love is a conditional, qualified love which looks for something lovable, desirable in the object of love. But that is not the way of God's love. The key verse that says it all is this one, "But God shows his love for us in that while we were yet sinners, Christ died for us." There is no expression of worth or value here that motivated God to spend Himself for us. Jesus gave Himself for the unlovely, unlovable and ungodly – for us.

Human love examines the attractive attributes of the other to look for something worth loving. The agape love of God seeks no such validation. God loves. Period. Such love is a stunning reversal of our way. God is deeply concerned with us and all our works and all our ways, but they do not serve as the basis for His love. In Christ, God loves us for no other reason than that He chooses to do so. That is His glory, and our hope.

Quid Pro Quo

The sixth chapter of Matthew's gospel contains a portion of what has been called the "Sermon on the Mount." In that chapter there are three verses in which Jesus speaks of praying, fasting and alms giving in secret. The King James translation, however, adds a word to the end of these verses. That word is 'openly.' The formula in which the word appears can be represented by verse 4, "...and thy Father which seest in secret shall reward thee openly."

Modern translations do not contain the word 'openly'. In fact the earliest manuscripts, from the second, third and fourth centuries upon which modern translations are based, do not contain the word openly. It was added at a later date. Why?

I believe it has something to do with the perpetual need to resolve the tension between hiddenness and openness in the Christian life. Consider this. Our society was profoundly shaped by what has been termed the 'Protestant ethic.' The Protestant ethic states simply, to use Matthew's words, if I pray, give alms and fast (as sincere acts of Christian piety) I will be rewarded with prosperity. Therefore you can tell who the serious Christians are by how prosperous their lives are. God openly rewards the sincerely pious. This permeates the Church like ink in the water. It is everywhere.

But a careful reading of the Sermon on the Mount (chapters 5-7 in Matthew) reveals that openness and hiddenness are in constant tension.

What all this means for me is that the Christian has no reason to expect that our living of the Christian life is going to be any more obvious than was Jesus' own life. For the world is not going to look at the Church and exclaim, "My you are so absolutely gorgeous, I must sign up. Count me in." Among the many implications of this awareness is one that stands apart. If the Church is going to bear witness to the faith, then it must speak the name of Jesus Christ and tell the story of what He has done for a sinful world. Attempts to resolve the tension within the Christian life only result in taking the focus off Jesus and placing it on ourselves. This we cannot and must not do.

Blues Lament

There is no perfect church, so don't waste your time looking for one. Jesus did not intentionally look for twelve guys who were dazed and confused to be his disciples. He did not have to. Dazed and confused is the default condition of humanity where God is concerned! Any twelve would have done nicely. It is sort of like a congregation choosing a church council, or a seminary fishing around for faculty. The only available candidates are sinners. So let us be clear: to be in the church is not to find some Archimedean point of ecclesiastical perfection beyond the taint of history where I am safely ensconced and where you can be also. The old adage I heard somewhere says it well: "The church is like Noah's ark. If it weren't for the storm outside one couldn't stand the stink inside." In fact, there are times when the storm outside seems preferable! In this respect I have often found more solace and camaraderie jamming among real sinners in a blues bar with my two sons than sipping coffee during the fellowship hour in the company of sinners who are convinced of their saintliness.

So while some may be whining and lamenting about the imperfections of "my church, my church, my dear old church," in the hopes of bringing back some long lost ideal fellowship, I am not one of them. The Church has always stumbled through time, unequal to the task set before it. I have no illusions about what a mess the Church is and will remain until our dear Lord rings in the kingdom.

But it is precisely because we are not up to the task that we can and do mishandle it, often very badly. Lutherans, perhaps more than any other Christian group, ought to be keenly aware of this. Our namesake, after all, gave "heart, soul, mind and strength" to confront a Church that had lost its voice for the Gospel. So, I want to add my voice to the chorus of those singing the blues, in the tradition of Brother Martin, over the state of a Church that is once again losing its voice for the Good News. And if you know anything about the blues, those earth-bound laments often stem from a hope and a longing that the ever-new, spirit-filled Word will create a new day. That is my hope too.

191

"...who were born, not of blood nor of the will of the flesh nor of the will of man, but of God." John 1:13

For many people, confrontational revivalism (the Gospel at gunpoint, as one called it) is assumed to be the default way in which the Church does evangelism. Give people a choice: heaven or hell, which will it be? Everyone must make a decision. First, accept Jesus as savior, then you must make Him Lord of your life. Salvation and this life are in some strange way unrelated, separated. Salvation becomes adherence to an ideology.

What we have going on here, it seems to me, is the religious equivalent of a sales pitch for a consumer decision about a product, rather than the proclamation of the decision God has made about sinners. And it is no accident that what has characterized these ministries from the 19th century up to the present is a reliance on the end justifying the means. All that matters is closing the deal. No method or gimmick is too outrageous, provided we can bring people to the point of decision. Then, once the decision has been made, the job is to keep the whip of spiritual growth on their backs so that Jesus will really become their Lord.

But since when does manipulation play a part in the open and free proclamation of God's grace? The only possible way to find any of this in the New testament is to "cherry pick" verses and bend them out of all shape and context.

The New Testament witness does not separate the saving work of Christ, His will to save from His will to be Lord. His Lordship and salvation are inseparable, because He is the one who has done the deciding. He has chosen you in Baptism. He is the one whose life now defines the life of the Christian and Christian community. The only will that is free to do any choosing where God is concerned is God's will. For us to claim such freedom is not the key to salvation, it is blasphemy. For it is claiming something for ourselves that belongs to God alone.

Evangelism, therefore, is being brought by God's grace – through Word and sacrament – to be with those whose great need is God's concern. To trust God, to believe the Gospel, is not a consequence of my decision, it is the form God's decision, born in faith, takes for me.

The Holy Spirit

Christians speak of the gift of the Holy Spirit. Lutherans believe the Spirit is given in Baptism. The Holy Spirit is not God in a different appearance, a different aspect of God, an alternate mode of appearing. What we are really saying is that the indivisible God is within us, is given to us.

Two points here are worth exploring. First, since the Holy Spirit is within us it is difficult to distinguish the presence of the Spirit from ourselves. I still experience myself as the principal subject. From here it is an easy step to interpret my thoughts, words and actions as those of the Holy Spirit. It is what lead Martin Luther to say of the radical reformers of the 16th century, "They have swallowed the Holy Spirit feathers and all!" The radicals believed that the Spirit was in them but they could not experience God as Someone apart from them.

This brings me to my second point. Does God want us to experience Him or encounter Him? It may seem like an odd question, but bear with me. The experience of the inner life and its emotions may be interpreted wildly and often are. If I equate the Holy Spirit with these feelings, emotions, etc. I may collapse God utterly into myself and anything goes.

But when I encounter the Spirit through Christ I am drawn outward to the external Word and the sacraments that I may rely upon God's promises given there, and to the neighbor as an encounter with Christ. "When you do it to the least of these, you do it to me." Then the presence of the Spirit, which the Word and the sacraments guarantee and which I encounter in my neighbors need, become indistinguishable from faith's power. And that power, which is really just another way saying God's power, in the freedom of faith turns us back into life so that we encounter the ordinary business of living for its own sake, and not as the occasion for experiencing the God whose glory, for now, is hidden from us.

Evangelical Freedom

Martin Luther was a conserving, but not a strictly conservative reformer. At times his writings emphasize continuity with the historic Church, insisting that if some traditions serve the faith of the people they should be retained. At other times the reformer freely slaughtered sacred cows that he believed were non-essentials.

Rooted in the principle of what has been called "evangelical freedom," Lutheran congregations are not obligated to any particular form. Our chief obligation is to the message of the Cross, the Good News that God justifies the ungodly. Because Lutherans also have (or should have) a clear-headed doctrine of sin, there is probably good reason for us to err on the side of tradition without becoming traditionalists. Order, even if imperfect and inefficient, is better than chaos.

Traditional church forms can provide stability in chaotic times, a framework for congregational mission and nurture, and a witness to our continuity with the historic Church. At the same time, evangelical freedom summons the congregation to place whatever forms it adopts at the service of the mission of the Gospel. Congregations are not private chaplaincies, country clubs for the like-minded. Congregations are mission outposts, always seeking to provide forms and forums through which the message of God's love for a lost and sinful world may gain the widest possible hearing.

No Empty Barking!

Professor James Nestingen once noted that In teaching them to pray, Jesus did not teach His disciples to transcend themselves, but to ask. And asking, of course, is something we humans are not very good at. Why? Because asking is a form of dying, a recognition of our limitations, an admission of need and a direct threat to our most dearly beloved, self-reliance.

When Jesus spoke of the life of faith He said things like this: "If anyone would find their life in this world, they must lose it." He spoke of denying self and taking up the cross. Dying must come before life can begin.

When Saint Paul wrote to the Romans he brought them back to baptism in order to make clear the dynamic of the Christian life: "Do you not know," he wrote, "that all of you who were baptized into Christ Jesus were baptized into His death?" The sinner, sickened by sin, is beyond remedy. The patient must die.

The Easter paradigm of the Christian life is not an invitation to transcend upward to ever greater heights of spirituality and success. This may be good humanism, but it is lousy Christianity, what Martin Luther called the Theology of Glory. Jesus was not raised from the dead in order to prop up our projects, however we define them. He was raised, as the New Testament proclaims "for our justification" (to establish sinners in a right relationship with God). It is for this reason that we can say with Saint Paul, "It is no longer I who live but Christ who lives in me."

Easter is not the occasion for a lot of empty religious barking about new life. Our lives and the world are not progressing they are coming to an end. The life we do live is a life of faith – not faith in what we have done or believed, but faith in Christ Jesus on whose cross my sinful self has met its end, and out of whose empty tomb reverberates the promise of eternity.

The Old, Old Story

Being a pastor in northern Minnesota means that you spend a lot of time sipping coffee with old Scandinavians. During those times, I learned a lot about the Christian faith. Here is some of what those folks taught their young pastor.

Faith in Jesus Christ and His promises was the marrow in their lives. And they had not come to this faith because some clergy person blathered on from the pulpit about the indelible wonderfulness of new and the novel, or about the benefits of being a radically inclusive, hyper-tolerant church. The message that gripped them was Gospel story of Jesus and His love for sinners. They loved to express their faith in their favorite hymns: Beautiful Savior, The Old Rugged Cross, Abide with Me, A Mighty Fortress is Our God , In the Garden among many others. The Bible and the Luther's Small Catechism came up again and again in our conversations.

During my years as their pastor, I had to bury some of those folks. Often, in the final days before the end, sitting by their bedsides, we would sing those old hymns, accompanied by my guitar, and read passages from the Bible. That is when they taught me something every pastor should know: if you can't sing it or say it at someone's deathbed, it probably isn't worth singing or saying at all.

All of this is to say that those folks encouraged me to resist the call to "get with it." They taught me something about what is truly relevant. They taught me that there is no substitute for the "old, old story of Jesus and His love."

For Our Benefit

There was a time in the Lutheran Church, when we baptized our babies and we celebrated grace and we sang the liturgy and sang the hymns and rejoiced in what God has given us in the sacraments. Nowadays, everybody is up in arms about sacraments. "Well...they can't be that gracious. You've got to do something" ...and we are right back in that paradigm of, "Well...what do I have to do to appropriate it...to make it my own?"

God did not wait for our assessment before He came into the world in the baby Jesus. "OK...who down there thinks this is a good idea...that I show up in Jesus Christ? Let me see a show of hands. Alright...I guess that is enough...I'll come." No. He came because He chose to come. He came even though He was not wanted. We read in John 1: "He came to his own people and his own people did not receive him." God is not waiting for us to decide something or to change our lives and get ourselves straightened out. He comes to us in the midst of our tangledness, our lostness, our confusion, our sin, our hurts, our hopes, our dreams...all the tangled up stuff of our lives...and He takes a hold of us right there in the middle of it. That is the gospel. He does not wait for us to make a decision. He makes the decision for us, for our benefit. This is a real challenging way of thinking about the faith for people today. Because we have all decided, one way or another, many of us, that, "Well, that's all well and good but we have to have the final say, somehow."

But grace is not a project. The sacraments, the Gospel, are not spiritual ideas for us to internalize and figure out. They come utterly from outside of us, asking nothing from us. They are given solely by His grace for our benefit, for the sake of Christ that our confidence may be in Christ. And, as Luther said, "in Christ alone."

Christ is the end of the law.

With the new year comes the time for resolutions. As we look back over the year that was, most of us can identify aspects of our lives that could use some improvement or adjustment. What strikes me about this annual exercise is that it never ends. Still, making resolutions can at least give one a sense of hope, if nothing else. I would like to hope, as each year rolls around, that some prospect exists for a remediation of life: lose weight, be more efficient in use of time, "smell the roses" a bit more often, and so forth.

Yet there is something more going on here that cuts deeply into the reality of life in God's world. Life is lived under the demands of God's law. You see, the apparently innocuous annual new year's resolution is actually a window into the reality of the human condition before God. We are bound to the law in all its forms and its absolute demands.

The law is always ahead of us with it's endless demands. At the same time Christ Jesus is even further ahead with His Cross and forgiveness. This is what the Bible means when it declares, "Christ is the end of the law."

So, make all the resolutions you want (Personally, I'm going for weight loss). Just remember that your life is already fulfilled in Jesus. Without Him, fulfilling our lives is a chimerical quest that never arrives. With Him we have it all!

"The darkness could not overcome it." John 1:5

The Temple of Vesta stands in the Roman Forum. The small, circular structure was among the most important buildings in all the Roman empire. A fire was kept burning there, 24 hours a day, for centuries. The keepers of this flame were a small group of women and girls who had been especially chosen. They were housed in a beautiful complex just behind the temple and for thirty years were devoted to this task. As long as the flame burned, Rome would endure.

Today, the flame to which the Romans devoted so much care and attention, has been extinguished. The compound of the Vestals, and the temple over which they kept watch, are in ruins. The Roman empire, seemingly destined to endure forever, is gone.

Christians, too, have a light which requires our attention. That light is the message of the Gospel, the Good News. From generation to generation, the Church is mandated to make the stewardship of the Word of God its first priority. Other matters may occupy our time and attention, but none are more important.

Unlike the flame of the Vestals, however, the light of Christ is not dependent upon us in order to endure. We do not keep the light of the Word alive, the Word keeps us alive. I take great comfort in this. For while the obligation to bear witness to the Word challenges me, I know that God provides all the necessary resources to make His Word known. God has chosen to keep His light burning not in beautiful marble temples but in earthen pots like you and me. God keeps the Word, Jesus our Lord, down to earth, in our hearts, on our lips, as near as a breath, as near as the sacraments, close to the hurts and hopes of the world. And in doing so He keeps us in the promise: the light of Christ will shine no matter how persistent the darkness may be.

Hope

To hope in Jesus Christ is to believe that the weights of time and temporal life have lost their power to crush us into meaninglessness. This is precisely the hope that Jesus held in His Father as He wept in the garden and hung on the bloody Cross. There is a new humanity coming. But as Christians we do not believe we will be led by one another along paths of our own making to a self-made future. We are held in faith by the One who struggled in this life, as we must, and who entered into death, as we will, which will bring all our plans to nothing.

Therefore, in the final analysis, our hope extends into the vast, empty topography of death. For our final hope is that even as we lay bound in death's cold grip we will hear our name, as the sheep knows the voice of the Shepherd. Then, like ancient Lazarus we will stumble from death into the light and life of the One who has promised,

"I give them eternal life, and they will never perish, and no one will snatch them out of my hand."

Made in the USA
San Bernardino, CA
15 December 2017